WHO DO YOU WANT TO BE TODAY?

Be inspired to dress differently

Trinny Woodall &
Susannah Constantine

Photography by Robin Matthews

PHOENIX
ILLUSTRATED

D1424155

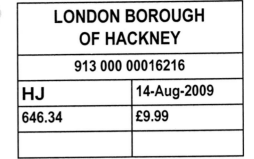
First published in Great Britain in 2008
by Weidenfeld & Nicolson
This edition published by Phoenix Illustrated in 2009
10 9 8 7 6 5 4 3 2 1

Text copyright © Trinny Woodall & Susannah Constantine 2008
Design and layout © Weidenfeld & Nicolson 2008

Photographs copyright © Robin Matthews 2008
For other photographs, see page 286

A CIP catalogue record for this book is available from the British Library.
ISBN: 978-0-7538-2626-3

Visit the girls at their website:
www.trinnyandsusannah.com

Printed in Italy

Phoenix Illustrated
The Orion Publishing Group Ltd
Orion House
5 Upper St Martin's Lane
London WC2H 9EA
www.orionbooks.co.uk

An Hachette UK company

Mixed Sources
Product group from well-managed forests and other controlled sources
www.fsc.org Cert no. CQ-COC-000012
© 1996 Forest Stewardship Council

FSC

Contents

Who do you want to be today?

This is a book to inspire the creative spirit in you.

We won't spend any time here explaining that a deep V will flatter a big bust or that slashed necklines help to balance saddlebags. If you haven't learned that yet, please go back and look at *The Body Shape Bible*. We are assuming that you might have read *What Your Clothes Say About You* and have broken free from allowing your wardrobe to define you. We trust that you have a basic grasp of colour and accessorising as explained in *What You Wear Can Change Your Life*. But if you don't yet have a degree from the Trinny & Susannah Style Academy, don't worry about it – just get stuck right in and have some fun with this book.

If you have been with us on our journey so far, you will know every angle and curve of your body shape and how to flatter it. You have been inspected, dissected, analysed and hopefully had your style confidence bolstered. You are already well on the way to being an expert in colour combining and in the alchemy of using pattern and texture to maximise your assets and minimise your flaws.

In short, you have a doctorate in the science of dressing. Now we turn your attention to the art thereof – the art of expressing yourself, the art of turning your wardrobe into an adventure playground, the art of putting yourself first.

Knowing the rules for your shape gives you the confidence and freedom to experiment. A great jazz artist gains a sound basic knowledge of music theory, but she doesn't then spend the rest of her days playing scales. She uses her training to take wing and express her individuality – to have fun.

To take the music analogy further…would you be satisfied by finding a record that you like and then playing it on all occasions: in the morning, in the car, at work and at parties? Of course not. We want music to suit our mood, to embellish the moment.

It's the same with clothes. Do you want to be flirty? Try the Bombshell. Feeling divine? Then dress as a Diva. For carefree days, the Boho look is perfect. Or if you feel the need to be in control, why not don the attire of the Sophisticate?

We're not suggesting that you choose to become a full-time Rock Chick, going in for hard drinking and a huge tattoo, but aren't there days when you would just love to outrage the neighbours and break some rules? Or perhaps you tire of continually being on the receiving end of intrusive chat-up lines and want to keep your distance today. You need to borrow the hauteur of the Ice Queen. But being regal can also become a trifle tiresome and now you just want to relax and have a laugh with the boys. So dress down as a stylish Androgyne.

Maybe your life seems a bit on the grey side, so try on the rose-tinted spectacles of a sugary sweet Gamine. You might want to parade about in the pampered persona of a High Maintenance babe, just to see if you can get away with it, or leave everyone staring as you sashay by in a striking Cutting Edge Cool outfit.

Are you just bored, bored, bored, of everything being so neat and predictable? Why not kick over the traces and outrage your family by swanning out in a wildly Avant-Garde Eccentric look? Or perhaps you're overwhelmed by the sheer chaos of life? It can feel really soothing to adopt the Zen-like persona of a calm, collected Minimalist.

No one expects you to go all the way and throw out your collection of china pigs, burn your frilly knickers and give your children matching raven-black

hairstyles. The point is to find the courage and inspiration to give it a go – just for one day. The pressures of daily life can take up all your time and energy. You have probably devised a set of outfits that flatter your body and are easy to wear – so you don't have to think about them anymore. And that's great…as far as it goes.

The truth is that it is so tempting to find a formula that suits us and then play it safe, wearing the same look month in and month out until it takes on the air of a uniform. But life, thank heavens, is not one endless Groundhog Day.

There are women who lean strongly toward one look or another. These style icons are your inspirations for dressing. Most of us, however, are happy to be more chameleon-like, adopting an outfit that will enhance our day *today*. In this book, we show you how to be all the women that you secretly desire to be. We want you to shine and be the star of your own show.

More than any of our previous books, this is about pure fun and frivolity. So dive in, get creative and indulge yourself. Be who *you* want to be today.

The starting point

While there is absolutely nothing wrong with how these women look, ask yourself, 'Will they turn heads?'

Are their outfits inspiring, fun, worthy or of note? We think you know the answer. The bland truth is that this is how most of us end up dressing, most of the time.

Pookie
Mid 20s
Size 10

Charlotte
Early 30s
Size 16

Natalie

Early 40s
Size 14

Rosamund

Late 50s
Size 12

Carrying it off with confidence

Congratulations, you are inspired to try a new style. You feel the resonance of the look, it sings to you. You've decided the occasion when you will give your new style an outing. Then, inevitably, doubts invade your mind. That negative gremlin is sitting on your shoulder crooning, 'You're going to make a fool of yourself. Are you auditioning for a pantomime? PEOPLE WILL LOOK AT YOU.' Well, of course people will look at you...that's the whole point.

The key to carrying off a bold new style is to step out with your head held high, knowing that you look great. You need to take a few preliminary steps to build up your confidence.

Make a mood board for your look. This is the first thing that the fashion houses do to establish the feel of their latest collection. Gather together photos of women who are style icons, pictures of inspirational works of art, scraps of patterns and fabric swatches. Tear out magazine photos of garments that you would love to wear. Glue, pin or Sellotape them all together onto a 'board of inspiration' and put it on your dressing table.

Watch films and listen to music to get you into the mood. There are inspiring suggestions in this book.

Don't rush to invest in an entirely new wardrobe. See what you have in your closet already. If you've been paying attention these last few years, it's likely that the clothes that you have will suit your body shape and colouring. Clever use of accessories is often all that's needed to completely change the style of an outfit.

Obviously it will be difficult to achieve, for example, the Diva style if your wardrobe exclusively consists of jeans, trainers and casual gear, or to stride out in the Androgyne style if your cupboard is stuffed full of flowery pink frills and petticoats. But there's still no need to go and blow the kids' inheritance at Dior. Experiment with a few cheap clothes from chain stores before you push the boat out.

The secret to self-confidence is to feel at ease in your style, to give the impression that you wear it every day. Wear your new look around the house, practise walking, sitting, lounging and eating in it. With a bit of prior rehearsal you will avoid those hideous moments of sudden realisation that you can't get down the street in those heels or you're not sure how to get out of the car in a mini skirt or that your sheath dress is so tight that you can't eat even a celery stick without bursting the seams.

If you're still feeling hesitant, wear your new style out to a place where nobody knows you. Pay attention to the reactions of strangers.

Surprise your children or partner with your new style. Hear what they say, but do be prepared to take it with a pinch of salt. There's no one more conservative and stick-in-the-mud than kids, and loved ones can often feel unsettled, even threatened, if you change your look and they suddenly see you in a new light.

Ask a friend to take some Polaroids or digital photos of you in your new style. Then tape them to the inside of your wardrobe door. These will be invaluable if you decide that you love the style and want to do it again in the future. It's surprising just how quickly you will completely forget how you put that fabulous look together.

Bombshell

You're hot and sassy

I JUST DON'T HAVE THE CURVES FOR BOMBSHELL STYLES.

So you want be a Bombshell today?

Bombshell – *'A stunningly attractive young woman'*.
OXFORD ENGLISH DICTIONARY

So, you want maximum male attention today. You feel ready to take wolf whistles on your dimpled chin and cause a car crash on the high street. You want heads to turn, to make people smile and generally be a small piece of happiness in the drudgery of everyday life. Hoorah for you. Today is the day for the Bombshell to emerge from beneath her down duvet, all tousled and cuddly. You feel sexy and malleable, soft and kissable. You need to capture this delicious confidence and wrap it up in some figure-hugging, curve-creating clothes.

So what is stopping you? 'But, but, but, I'm too old…My boyfriend will KILL me…No one will take me seriously, for goodness sake…I have brown hair…No time, no clothes, no tits…No confidence.'

While a total lack of bosom is a handicap (Trinny would never do this look), all the rest is naught but excuses. Worthy excuses, but excuses nonetheless. You can turn the sexy dial up and down to fit your mood or the shape of your day. After all, the Bombshell isn't only about lusciousness. She also has an air of innocence, a kittenish sweetness that is totally unthreatening and ultimately appealing. So switch the shower for a bath full of bubbles and let your curls down. Get into the mood by watching *And God Created Woman* with Brigitte Bardot or *Gentlemen Prefer Blondes* starring that exemplary Bombshell – Marilyn Monroe. Play a Rufus Wainwright CD and dance around singing into your hairbrush. It's boring being taken seriously all the time.

The title 'Bombshell' encapsulates the sizzling innocence that was Marilyn and her wiggling blonde disciples: Jayne Mansfield and Diana Dors. Many have followed in those kitten-heeled footsteps. Dolly Parton has given us the cowgirl version, a rhinestone rodeo with zeppelin boobs. Younger Bombshells are led by Scarlett Johansson, rarely out of satin on the red carpet. Her bosoms burst forth from tightly corseted dresses as she smiles provocatively through crimson lips. Alison Goldfrapp has taken the Bombshell into the twenty-first century with an other-worldly quality that inspires many a young man's fantasy.

It is simply impossible to achieve the Bombshell look if you start with a wardrobe full of combat trousers and fleeces. An accomplished Bombshell requires fitted, figure-hugging, saucy and overtly suggestive clothing. You have one toe in Soho and the other in the playground.

Make no mistake – to be a Bombshell you need to be feeling really GREAT about yourself. Her royal Bombshellness is always on parade and ready to pop out of a birthday cake at any given moment. She isn't fazed by seeming approachable to EVERYONE. The joy of the Bombshell is that she is equally liked by men and women, albeit for different reasons. The boys want to bed her and the girls want to be her best friends. Strangers will approach you and kids will want to hold your hand. If you pull off the look effectively you're in a win-win situation.

Take it from Marilyn, Brigitte and Scarlett…Bombshells have much more fun.

Bombshell wardrobe essentials

Clothes

- PENCIL SKIRTS
- PEDAL PUSHERS
- WAISTCOATS
- FITTED, SHORT JACKETS
- TIGHT, KNITTED TOPS
- FULL-LENGTH GOWNS

Colour, pattern and texture

- LEOPARD PRINT
- NARROW STRIPES
- FAKE FUR
- SATINS
- SEQUINS
- LOTS OF PINK

Take design inspiration from

- VIVIENNE WESTWOOD
- DOLCE & GABBANA
- ALEXANDER MCQUEEN
- BLUMARINE
- NANETTE LEPORE

Daytime Bombshell

A Bombshell never really does casual. If you could go to the picnic in the park dressed in gold lamé and white marabou, you surely would.

Boring old convention requires, however, that on occasion you tone it down. The idea is, we guess, to give other women a look in, at school sports day, for instance, or even just down at the local greengrocer. As a Bombshell, you manage to look just as head turning at 2 p.m. as you do at midnight.

Tops

A t-shirt isn't a big old square sack. It's stretchy and figure sculpting. Bombshell clothes must work every curve you've got. Narrow stripes create a curvy illusion through optical distortion. Tiny polka dots or a small floral pattern also have a softening effect.

Play up your waist

Always, always, make the most of your waist. Winch it in with corsets, wrap it in belts, carve it with big buttons…a Bombshell does not do 'boxy'. Nor does she do baggy pants.

Pedal pushers

Stopping just below the knee, pedal pushers accentuate the slimmest part of your leg creating the illusion of a curvier calf.

Shoes

If you can't flash your diamonds during the day, then you must dazzle with a flash of gorgeous ankle. The boyish Gamine might paddle around in flat pumps. You, a true Bombshell, require heels at all times.

'Create
fabulous
curves at
all times
of the day.'

'At night, the
Bombshell
brings out
her big
guns.'

Night-time Bombshell

While your daytime look is fun, your night-time look is only just this side of legal. It's all about wiggle, the wobble, the woo-woo-woo!

Cleavage

Create cleavage. Even if you have to empty your boyfriend's sock drawer to do it. Use chicken fillets, wear padded, push-up, pull-in, hoik-em-high bras. The bosom is the Bombshell's first asset.

Lingerie

Sexy underwear is your best investment. Always find a way to show a flash of lacy bra edge, whether it's a button that you dizzily forgot to fasten or a cheekily dropped shoulder strap.

Hug your bum

Make sure your clothes create curves everywhere. You are a Bombshell round the back as well. Wrap that backside tightly and then drop your hanky. Listen to the whole room hold their breath while you retrieve it. If you are not naturally well endowed in the bottom department, a pair of Magic Knickers are definitely required. Dresses with frills or a small pelmet across the butt also work wonders. That way you will make just as much impact going as you do coming.

High heels

Your heels must be high. To get that Bombshell wiggle, practise walking in a straight line, as if on a tightrope. It doesn't matter if you teeter a bit. A Bombshell is never perfect.

Bombshell finishing touches

When it comes to trinkets and fluff, you must go completely over the top. Bombshell accessories have a sparkly air of frivolity. You want to have it all, and so you shall. Put together, these touches will bring out your inner Bombshell and give you the confidence to be playfully sexy.

Bombshell looks are perfectly set off by the shine of gold leather.

A bit of white fake fur will make you look cute as a bunny (the Playboy variety, naturally).

Always contrive to flash a bit of gorgeous lace-clad cleavage.

Diamonds are girl's best friend but, hey, piles of diamantés look great too.

Your shoes are cute, but always with high heels.

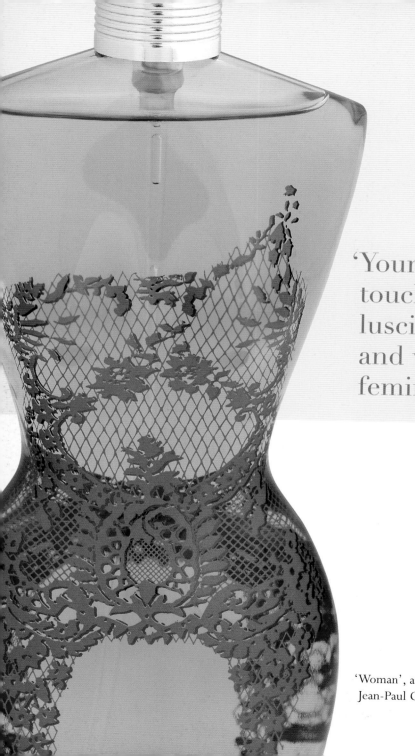

'Your finishing
touches are
luscious, sexy
and very
feminine.'

'Woman', a scent by
Jean-Paul Gaultier.

Fine hairspray is essential for maintaining your casually tousled big hair.

A Bombshell always feels powdered and pampered.

Fire-engine red lips and nails will get those alarm bells ringing.

LE VERNIS
NAIL COLOUR

159
FIRE

CHANEL

Bombshell beauty

The Bombshell is all about lips and lashes. You're not going for a rosy milkmaid look. It's a sexy, tousled, come-to-bed effect that, unfortunately, is not as easy to achieve as just falling out of bed. This look takes effort, but the head-turning result is well worth it.

Start with gorgeous, radiant skin. Use a foundation with a little bit of added glow. Sculpt your cheeks with two powder blushers. Use a darker, neutral colour underneath the cheekbones, then pop a tiny flush of lighter colour actually on your cheekbone. Blend the two.

Your brows should be strongly defined. Strengthen them with a brow powder. Shape neatly to a pointed end with good brow brush.

Keep your eyes very clean. Use a neutral flesh colour all over the lid, up to your brow and right into the corner. Bright, pearly white eyeshadow will make you look like a fancy dress version of Marilyn. We suggest something warm and peachy. Apply a smoky grey shadow closely along the outer third of your eyelid and smudge it with a rounded brush. Then use a thin angled brush to add a stronger line over the top of that so that you end up with a line that is well defined but softer than an eyeliner. Leave underneath your eyes free of shadow.

Curl your lashes to within an inch of their lives. Apply very black mascara, working it right up from the roots of the lashes. Finally, add a few individual false lashes at the outer edges of your eyes for extra flair.

Every self-respecting Bombshell needs an eyeliner pencil. Not to line your eyes, but to apply that one strategic, sexy beauty spot – midway between the curl of your lip and the flare of your nostril. Make sure that it is a believable colour for your skin tone.

Apply the brightest, pillar-box red lipstick you can find, in four layers. Carry your lipstick in your handbag and reapply it often, preferably using a crystal-studded compact mirror.

How to do the Bombshell look

Luscious lips

To make your lipstick last all day, start with a good primer as a base.

Use a lip-wax pencil around your lip line to stop any colour bleeding.

Using a small brush, dot concealer around the rim of your lips. Brush it in to smooth out the shape of your lip line.

Using a lip brush, start by painting in your Cupid's bow, then do the centre of your bottom lip and finally fill the colour in from the sides. Blot your lips with a tissue and repeat, building the colour up in two, three or four layers.

Bombshell curls

- Make your hair as soft and luxurious as possible. Start with a smoothing shampoo.

- Turn your head upside down and blast your hair, pushing it forwards with a paddle brush to give you volume at the roots. This is a look that requires lots of product. Use a volumising fluid at the roots and a gutsy mousse all over.

- When your hair is dry, use hot rollers – the smaller ones around the back and front (the under layer) and the biggest ones in the middle (the top of your head).

- Finish the look with a shining serum. Rub a little on your hands and just run them lightly over the very top layers of your hair.

- For evenings, hold the look in place with hairspray.

Gamine

You're innocent and childlike

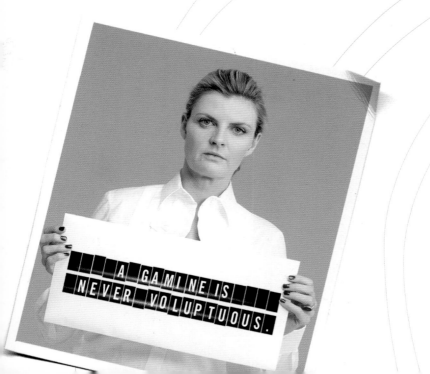

A GAMINE IS NEVER VOLUPTUOUS.

So you want be a Gamine today?

Gamine – *'A girl with a mischevious, boyish charm'*.
<small>OXFORD ENGLISH DICTIONARY</small>

It's a tough old world. People are pushing and shoving, ducking and diving. There is so much aggression in the air, so much unhappiness, poverty and strife. Most of the time you don't notice, being able to move through your day without it piercing your consciousness. But you are fully aware of those less fortunate. And you *do* care. You care a lot about world strife. Like the rest of us, you have had to toughen up somewhat to get on.

Friends and colleagues may take you as being a bit of a hard nut, but that is not how you really are. Not all the way through anyway. The time has come to let your guard down. You cry watching *The Sound of Music* and nearly crash each time you swerve to avoid flattening a road-crossing rabbit. You want people to be aware of your soft side and today you have decided that you are not afraid to show your vulnerability.

'But if I show my "weakness" I will get trampled on,' we hear you wail. There is a difference between weakness and honesty. By showing your feelings you are being true to your self and to those you love. 'All well and good, but how on earth can empathy be shown in clothing?' This, girls, is the easy part. Start by watching *Breakfast at Tiffany's* starring Audrey Hepburn and *Amélie* with Audrey Tatou. There are some other great role models to guide you – Edie Sedgwick, Mia Farrow and the wonderful Jackie Kennedy. There is nothing sexual about the way they dressed. Their style turned innocence into a gentle elegance that now has the international stamp of sweetness. And you can't think of Natalie Imbruglia or Winona Ryder without assuming they are utterly adorable.

We imagine them planting daffodils in their window boxes before skipping off to make a donation to the local donkey sanctuary. We can see them sipping camomile tea out of a porcelain cup and placing the tea bag in a precisely organised home-recycling system. Being Gamine is as easy as carrying a shopping basket to your local grocery (you don't condone big supermarket chains) and filling it with organic fruit and veg.

Becoming Gamine isn't the easiest thing for a buxom girl, for the simple reason that shift dresses and button-up princess collars look dreadful over anything other than a washboard chest. But if you are small breasted, this a fabulous look for you to concoct. Innocence is the key word here. Flower prints, big buttons and sunglasses will make you look waif-like, and pretty shoes and ballet pumps will give girly glamour a serious leg up.

The great thing about this air of fragility is that everyone will want to look after you. They will think you can't lift a suitcase or get angry with anyone. Men will leap to your defence – making them feel like Knights of the Round Table. If you want something done, flutter your Bambi eyelashes and you will have hundreds of willing helpers. Take a break from having to do and be it all to everyone.

Time to put up your dainty shell pink tootsies and watch the world waft by.

Gamine wardrobe essentials

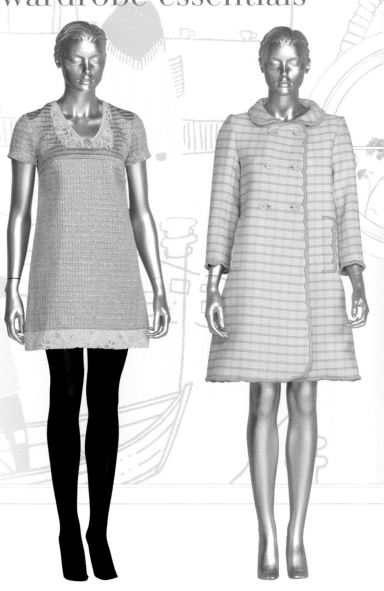

Clothes

- ◆ LITTLE BLACK DRESSES
- ◆ TULIP SKIRTS
- ◆ ROUND-COLLAR BLOUSES
- ◆ TUNIC DRESSES
- ◆ DUFFEL COATS
- ◆ CAPRI PANTS
- ◆ SHORT JACKETS

Pattern and texture

- ◆ BIG BUTTONS
- ◆ HOUNDSTOOTH CHECK
- ◆ PIN TUCKS
- ◆ BOX PLEATS
- ◆ GINGHAM
- ◆ POLKA DOTS

Take design inspiration from

- ◆ MARNI
- ◆ MARC JACOBS
- ◆ CHLOÉ
- ◆ COURRÈGES

Daytime Gamine

The Gamine look is neat, sweet and petite. You are vulnerable, girly and feminine in a playful way. Your look relies on shape and colour rather than obvious labels.

Blouse

A white cotton blouse with a pretty collar is the backbone of the Gamine's wardrobe. She usually teams it with a neat knitted cardigan or sweater.

Skirts

Gamine clothes always have a little girl quality. Skirts are flared or A-line, never bottom-hugging.

Necklines

Necklines are high and buttoned up. Somewhere between Madeleine and Minnie Mouse.

Dresses

Every Gamine needs a cute tunic dress. The skirt is flared and the hemline should be just above the knee.

Accessories

When the sun peeps out, enhance your fragile doll appearance with a pair of huge round sunglasses. Belts are delicate and slim. Find them in a vintage market to be sure that nobody else has the same one.

Legs

Complete the look with bare legs, opaque tights or over-the-knee socks.

Shoes

A Gamine girl cannot skip to the park in spiked heels or Doc Martens – no, no. The perfect Gamine footwear is a pair of flat ballet pumps.

'Gamine is neat
and cute as
a button.'

'The look is
sexy, yet in a
sweet and
innocent kind
of way.'

Night-time Gamine

At night, the Gamine grows up. You are still delicate and girly, but your chic dressing invokes an air of mystery. You never show off your cleavage, but rather use your arms to convey your feminine charms.

Dress

If in doubt, dig out the LBD. The Little Black Dress is such an important item in a Gamine's wardrobe that it even has its own time-saving acronym.

Coat

You love a cute coat, whether it was your grandmother's, a fabulous find at a vintage market or just a smart buy on the high street. It's usually in wool, flared and never longer than knee length.

Handbag

Your handbag doesn't scream 'Look at me'. Nor does it contain the kitchen sink. It is always understated, small and complements your dress.

Jewellery

Keep your jewellery small and simple. A pair of delicate earrings helps to make your head appear more prominent and your neck more slender and fragile. Tie your hair back to show them off.

Shoes

Strappy spike heels, gold decals and diamanté studs are not for you. Avoid flashy shoes. The Gamine always prefers a round toe, whether it is high or low.

Gamine finishing touches

The Gamine look is as sweet and pretty as a bag of mixed lollies. Pull your look together with these adorable accessories and beauty products.

What could be sweeter than a charm bracelet or delicate name bracelet?

Large round sunglasses create a Gamine air of fragility.

A beret is perfect for the classically Parisian Gamine look in colder months.

Skip through the day in flat pumps or sandals.

A wide Alice band is great for reinforcing the impression that the closest you get to a bar is at ballet class.

Like everything else about your look, your handbag is cute.

Play up your eyes
with long, thick
black lashes.

Your body should
feel, as well as
look, adorable.

Gamine nails are
neatly trimmed
and naturally pink.

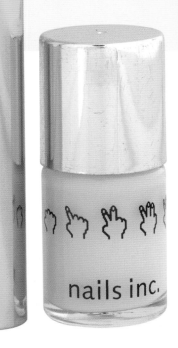

'Your scent should be light and fresh as a breath of springtime.'

'Miss Dior Chérie',
a scent by Dior.

Gamine beauty

All humans are instinctively drawn to the big head and wide eyes of a baby. A Gamine's look evokes youthful softness and approachability. You are a pretty, sweet girl who's fun to be with.

Gamine hair is always tidy but never expensively 'done'. Keep it simple in a bob or ponytail. A comb and an Alice band are essentials in the Gamine kit bag. On rainy, windswept days, protect your hair with a headscarf or a tiny fold-up red umbrella.

If you're not already perfect, then invest in a good foundation and concealer to create a flawless base. Gamine is a dewy, young look so don't cake on the powder. Your eyebrows should be tidy, but not overplayed.

When it comes to eyeshadow, you want to create a wide, round-eyed look, so think Bambi rather than vixen. Keep the colour really clean and neutral in tones that complement your skin. Your lips need to be pale to fix all the focus on your big doe eyes.

Warm up your face with a soft, baby colour applied just to the apples of your cheeks.

At night, use darker, smokier eyeshadows and really go to town with your lashes. Start with an eyelash-enhancing base and then add a good few layers of mascara, top and bottom. Add extra-long false eyelashes all the way from the outer to the inner corner of your eye for maximum batt-ability.

How to do the Gamine look

Twisted ponytail

Pull your hair straight back and high on the back of your head. Then give the ponytail a little twist with hot tongs, just to give it a bit of bounce. Tong all in the same direction so that it falls into one big curl.

Girly fringe

If you want a more Gamine look but you don't have a fringe, use a fake! Cut a triangular section from a hairpiece. Sweep your hair straight back into a ponytail, place the false fringe where your natural fringe would start and then pin the apex. Cover the join with a wide elasticated headband.

How to create Bambi eyes

The idea is to give you an air of wide-eyed innocence. Use a soft brush to apply a neutral, flesh-coloured eyeshadow all over your eyelid almost up to the brow or even right up to the brow (experiment to see which looks best on you).

Then blend a darker neutral tone into the outer third of your eye socket and blend it upward onto the brow bone.

Add a third, still darker, neutral colour only in the crease of your eye.

Curl your lashes and apply mascara top and bottom.

Finally, apply concealer underneath your eye, starting from the inner corner and working all the way around to the outer corner.

cuttingedgecool

you're original and experimental

So you want be Cutting Edge Cool today?

Cutting Edge Cool – *'Innovative and pioneering' and 'fashionably attractive'*.
<small>OXFORD ENGLISH DICTIONARY</small>

Have you ever been swept over by a secret desire to be cool, hip and trendy, but have absolutely no idea how to get there? Have you longed for the wow factor…to have the admiration of your girlfriends and be the envy of all your enemies? Then it's time for you to go Cutting Edge Cool, and slice through pedestrian dressing with hard core, forward-thinking fashion that will turn you from one of many to a one-off.

This is not easy and it takes dinosaur's balls to carry it off in a natural I-have-the-unique-gene manner. This we grant you. Susannah has a problem with this one because she feels too old and too busty to risk high fashion. It took half a day for her to get used to and actually kind of love her 'but I feel like a New Age bat' caped crusader look. It is especially hard if you are coming from a base camp of flowery skirts and twin sets. Expecting yourself to take the leap from worn-out mum to fashion trapeze artist is a bit like asking a mole to sky dive. Cutting Edge Cool may not be for the faint hearted. The timid and unconfident ones among you might be better trying on Gamine, Boho or Sophisticate for size before flinging yourself headlong into a perilous vat of ultra-cool dressing.

Once you have steeled yourself to go for it, there may be no turning back. Cutting Edge Cool is an art form that turns the individual doing it into a walking installation. Bjork is a work of art, as is Gwen Stefani. They are bold and completely unique to the point that anyone trying to copy their style would be a cheap imitation because their looks have been created solely by and for them. Then you get a starburst like Agyness Deyn. This young model has created a Cutting Edge Cool style that is accessible. Fashion follows HER, as do a legion of young fashion fans. These women are fearlessly experimental. Someone like Chloë Sevigny will latch on to the newest, most daring catwalk

look and take it down the red carpet. No duchess satin ball gowns for her. EVER. It's vintage or something so unlikely that one gasps at her sheer nerve. What a cool heroine!

Still up for it? Great! So now, down to the practicalities. Brush up on all the latest cool magazines (they change all the time so a trip to a specialist newsagent or an art bookshop is in order). Get into the mood by watching Robert Altman's film *Prêt-à-Porter*. You cannot and must not be seen driving a people carrier. If you have no alternative, take public transport. The juxtaposition of this madly modish individual sitting on a gum-encrusted bus bench is fabulous. Never be seen in the same outfit twice…clothes are your life and you are far too inventive not to have the imagination to mix and match another little creation from what is already in your wardrobe. It's great to have a few key pieces from hot designers, but if you do have the money to buy these, for goodness sake be sure you acquire nothing that has been on the back of a footballer's wife. It will kill your credibility quicker than a date with James Blunt. Check out new designers at markets and at the summer graduate shows of fashion colleges. Anything goes for Cutting Edge Cool just so long as it isn't conventional and is totally original. This opens the door to re-arranging clothes in your wardrobe into mad partnerships. Tutus with tailored jackets. Boy clothes with girl clothes. Be your own designer.

Have fun and take courage because, boy, will you stand out. Good luck!

POST CARD

RBA Awards

Cutting Edge Cool wardrobe essentials

Clothes

- THERE ARE NO RULES. JUST MAKE SURE IT'S HOT AND NOT WIDELY AVAILABLE. MIX IT UP AND MAKE IT YOUR OWN!

Colour, pattern and texture

- METALLIC PRINTS
- SPACE AGE FIBRES
- PLASTICS
- NEON
- CLASHING COLOURS

Take design inspiration from

- IMITATION OF CHRIST
- VIKTOR AND ROLF
- ANTONIO BERADI
- VINTAGE STORES

Cutting Edge Cool

The Cutting Edge Cool woman is an incredibly adventurous spirit. You are always in the vanguard and, as fashions change, so you move on – always staying a jump ahead of the pack. There are no rules or regulations about how to dress, no defining by day or by evening. Just be there first and claim the look as your own. The secret to successful Cutting Edge Cool dressing is in your attitude, your pose, your posture and most of all your confidence and faith in your outfit.

Mixing

An observer might think, 'How the hell do those go together?' That neon bag with a black belt and grey shoes! It breaks all the rules, but that's what Cutting Edge Cool is about.

Go into your wardrobe and challenge yourself. Pick up a bunch of things that you would never normally mix and see how you can make three of them work together. Unlike Minimalist where one thing dominates, with a Cutting Edge Cool look at least three items are fighting for attention, but pick the strongest to play up your best feature. A spotted skirt with a check jacket and a purple belt? Fabulous!

Always wear the wildest garment on the best part of your body. If you have great legs, for example, you can carry off these shocking pink footless tights.

New designers

We can never instantly identify where Cutting Edge Cool clothes come from. Seek out hip, new designers and then wear their clothes until they become recognisable. Then drop them like a hot brick. Some high street shops regularly feature capsule collections by new, young designers. Get inspiration from the Graduate Exhibition at your local College of Fashion which takes place every summer and showcases design talent from the UK's major fashion and textile universities: www.gfw.org.uk

'Challenge
yourself to
create an
exciting look
from wildly
clashing
elements.'

'Base your
outfit around
a garment
that flatters
your shape.'

Cutting Edge Cool

If you have a voluptuous figure, there is no reason why you can't do Cutting Edge Cool. The art is to wear a central garment that flatters your figure, then add wild tights, shoes and a belt. Remember to emphasise your best body part with a really figure-flattering piece.

Dressing up a key piece

Start with the one key piece that flatters your shape, whether it be a hip new designer garment or a vintage collector's item and mix it up with a mad handbag and cool shoes. Remember it is never about matching or being neat or restrained. You don't look like you got dressed in a hurry, but equally you don't want to look like you spent the day trying too hard to achieve your look. Ultimately your outfit might encompass items from Primark to Louis Vuitton, but you will always build it around that one utterly Cutting Edge piece.

It's important that your hair works well with your outfit. For example, take a pair of skinny jeans and instead of teaming it with the predictable smock dress and long cardigan, wear it with a 1970s Bill Gibb coat and a pair of 1990s shoes from a charity shop. Add a belt from Topshop.

If you left your hair scrunched up in a ponytail, you might just look badly dressed, but the crowning glory of a short, sharp bob (courtesy of a wig) pulls the whole look together and makes it work.

Charity stores and antique shops

Face it, fashion is endlessly cyclical. Everyone thinks that coat, handbag or belt is old hat, except you. You are so far out on the crest of the wave that you are catching the tide coming back in. So you can make great finds in charity shops, snaffling up the coming trend before anyone else is on to it. Small antique shops (not specialist vintage clothing stores) will also often have a rail of clothing oddities that are the source of many unique finds.

Cutting Edge Cool
finishing touches

Your accessories are razor sharp, just like you. Try putting pieces together in unexpected ways and mix eras and styles with artful abandon – a green belt with an orange bag, a 1980s hat with next year's shoes.

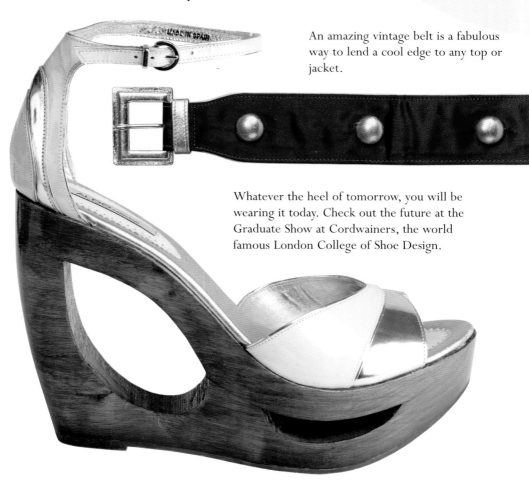

An amazing vintage belt is a fabulous way to lend a cool edge to any top or jacket.

Whatever the heel of tomorrow, you will be wearing it today. Check out the future at the Graduate Show at Cordwainers, the world famous London College of Shoe Design.

Cutting Edge Cool always chooses
stand-alone sunglasses.

Accessories are a great way to bring a high
fashion twist to your existing wardrobe.
Look out for hats that have personality.

Cutting Edge Cool is as much about
how you put your look together
as it is about each item. Dare
to mix clashing colours
and prints.

Cutting Edge Cool is not afraid to go to
extremes. You take bright and
boldly patterned leg wear
in your stride.

Well-chosen, eye-catching
jewellery is never out of
fashion. Wear it as a
statement piece rather
than piled on.

Your make-up always looks strong, but casually applied. Cosmetic colour is used to play up your outfit rather than your features.

'Cutting
Edge Cool
is not
afraid of
strong
colours.'

'Truly', a scent by Stephen Burlingham.

Cutting Edge Cool beauty

Cutting Edge Cool is always a strong and well-defined look. You have a sharp hair *cut*, not a style. It is about texture, colour and form. It might be messy and roughed up, strongly dyed or short with defined shape – it's a reflection of your purposeful character. But it's not always feasible to cut off all your hair or dye it blue just for the day, so use a wig to change the colour and style as you please. There are plenty of fun, synthetic wigs available for £20 or £30. Try different colours – platinum, black, red or purple.

Take the wig to your hairdresser and ask to have it cut it into a strong shape. It will cost the same as a professional haircut, but then you will always have a fabulous, funky hairstyle at your fingertips, with no work at all. If your hair is long, tuck it up in a wig cap first (it looks like the toe of a stocking and can be purchased from any wig store or large pharmacy).

While you are a make-up lover, it is not the cornerstone of your look. You choose make-up to highlight your cool outfit. If you are wearing day-glo tights, then you might go for day-glo fingernails. Or choose a slick of fuchsia lipstick to offset your fuchsia shoes, or add a flash of turquoise on your top eyelid with a waterproof pencil.

You don't bother with perfecting every contour or blending every shade, you might have painted your nails bright pink last week and then just let them get chipped. Often you will purposefully leave some feature completely blank, not done.

Everything comes together to create an impression of colour, inspiration and artful casualness.

How to do the
Cutting Edge Cool look

Enhance your eye colour

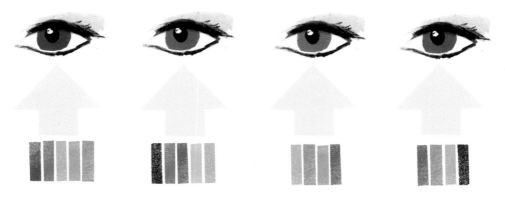

Experiment with rich colour to flatter both the shape of your eyes and the colour of your outfit.

Tip: 'Your wicked eye pencil should have a soft, smudgy
      consistency. Try it first on the back of your hand to
      make sure that it doesn't scratch your skin.'

Take your wig to the salon

ANDROGYNE

You're a girl in boy's clothing

So you want to be an Androgyne today?

An androgynous person — *'partly male and partly female in appearance'*.

OXFORD ENGLISH DICTIONARY

There are occasions in a woman's life when it serves her well to kick arse. Times when you must draw on the manly Marlene Dietrich gene to give yourself that extra edge required to handle a difficult situation. Sometimes we rise at the dawn of a new day thinking, 'I'm going to be the boss.' No more pussyfooting around, no more being pushed about. You want to be taken seriously and respected for your intellect. You feel more *Newsnight* than *Richard and Judy*. More Katharine Hepburn than Doris Day. Just for a while you want to bin the Marigolds and step free from the female stereotype.

Girl meets boy. Girl nicks a few fashion tips from boy and takes on a don't-mess-with-me attitude that gives her the freedom to speak her mind... charmingly, but uncensored and in no uncertain terms. Blurring your sexuality by sharpening soft curves gets you noticed in a way that commands respect from both sides of the feminist fence.

The joy of girl becomes boy is that men will be ever so slightly intimidated and confused, and women will applaud your balls and want to take a feather from your cocked Helmut Lang cap.

So, what's stopping you, hmmm? Are your nails too long and French polished? Don't tell us...your boobs dominate your body and you simply CANNOT leave the house without full make-up.

You know, it's not so hard to trim your nails and tone down the war paint. The boobs are an issue, but hey, look at a woman like Jamie Lee Curtis...all tits, arse and legs — a perfect doll body with an attitude and dress sense that tells us instantly that she wears the trousers. Androgyne icons like Cate Blanchett, Annie Lennox and Hilary Swank are admired for their fearlessness, be it with a cause they take up or roles they take on. Their boldness is reflected in their no-nonsense, frill-free style. If you are not sure how to achieve that fine masculine-feminine balance, rent a DVD of *Bringing up Baby* starring Katharine Hepburn. Get into the mood by reading the *Financial Times* or listening to some smooth jazz while downing a couple of straight-up Martinis.

Go on, give in to your masculine calling today. If you want to take charge of your life, start by empowering yourself with a little power suiting.

pull off the look effectively you're in a win-win situation... and can
wrap it...

It is sim...
hoodie...
have or...

The tit...
Mans...
cowgi...
Youn...
from...
Bo...

M...
f...

Androgyne wardrobe essentials

Clothes

- MEN'S SUITS
- TUXEDO DRESSES
- MEN'S SHIRTS
- WHITE T-SHIRTS
- WAISTCOATS
- COLUMN-LIKE EVENING DRESSES
- BELOW-THE-KNEE PENCIL SKIRTS

Colour, pattern and texture

- PINSTRIPES
- FLANNEL
- DARK NEUTRAL COLOURS
- BLACK AND WHITE
- PINTUCKS
- PLAIN COLOURS
- BEADING

Take design inspiration from

- HELMUT LANG
- JIL SANDER
- YVES SAINT LAURENT
- MARTIN MARGIELA
- SAVILE ROW

Daytime Androgyne

The art of Androgyne dressing is to steal men's style and make it your own. You are not a man, but you are smart and able to play them at their own game. Your masculine look always has a feminine twist. Wear a dress that's made from pinstripe suiting with super-high heels, or a man's suit and flat shoes with a pussy-bow blouse. The trick is to keep everyone guessing.

Trouser suits

A masculine cut is important. The younger you are, the more fitted and sharp your suit can be. If you are older, choose a more floppy, soft and forgiving suit. Always wear your suit with a shirt or a white t-shirt, never with a jumper. Your shoes are masculine, flat and they cover your toes – anything from a brogue to a Converse trainer.

White shirts

An Androgyne needs the perfect white shirt. One thing about white shirts is that, frankly, after thirty wears they lose their crispness and start to look a trifle grey and tired. Your white shirt must be crisp and sharp. Reasonably priced white shirts can be found at boys' school outfitters, but always get them tailored to fit your waist. Sometimes, though, it is worth investing in a fabulous designer white shirt.

Hats

A sharp suit needs a smart hat. Wear it at a jaunty tilt or pull it down over one eye. Androgyne hats are either very masculine or very floppy and feminine, but always with absolutely no embellishment.

Accessories

Keep accessories to a bare minimum: a watch, a tie, cufflinks. Your handbag should be a simple, no-nonsense leather clutch, free of logos, dangly heart keychains, embroidery or any other superfluous ornamentation. Make sure that you remember to lose that sweet locket chain and those pearl stud earrings that you unconsciously wear every day.

'Choose a suit
that will flatter
your shape.'

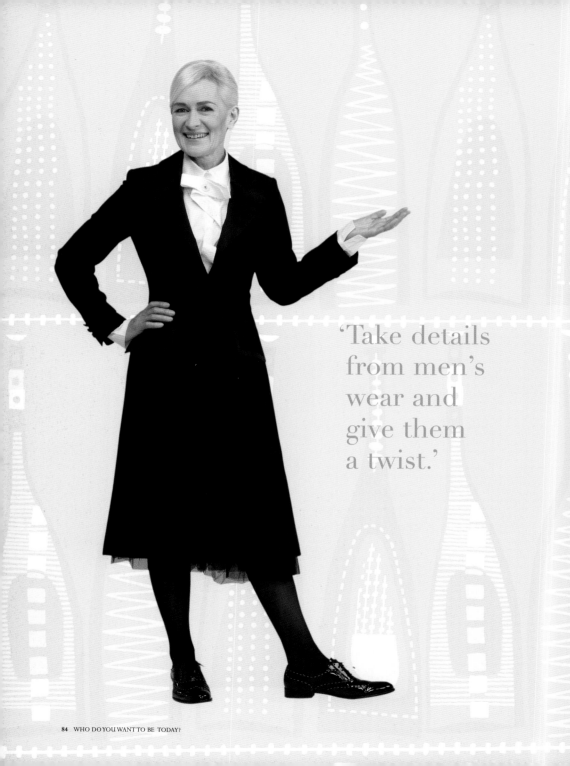

'Take details
from men's
wear and
give them
a twist.'

Night-time Androgyne

If you think you are too womanly to do an Androgyne look, just take a glance at Susannah on the opening page of this chapter. She has managed to keep her curviness while pulling off a totally streamlined androgynous style. Remember that as an Androgyne you are not trying to look butch, rather you are exuding self-confidence. The Androgyne doesn't need male attention – but she generally gets it.

Black and white

Your evening wardrobe consists almost entirely of black and white. To carry it off you must always be sure to create sharp, uncluttered lines in your outfits. Keep it clean and simple with only the occasional glimpse of metal or diamanté. And don't introduce any colour – it will kill the look.

Influences from men's evening wear

At night, your full glamour look borrows its finish from men's evening wear – for example, pin tucks, a silk waistcoat, a stiff white shirt, mother-of-pearl cufflinks or the braces on Susannah's skirt on page 75.

Feminine touches

Even though you take most of your style influences from menswear you manage to maintain femininity through little details. Poking out of Rosamund's tuxedo coat is a tiny bit of tulle, and although Susannah wears braces they are diamanté studded to give her look a twinkle. Trinny (on page 75) is wearing a beautiful statement necklace over her otherwise ultimately masculine look. Make sure that your feminine detailing is suitably sharp – a little string of pearls or a pale pink Pashmina wrap would not work.

Androgyne finishing touches

The Androgyne look is all about the twist – is she or isn't he?
Masculine accessories look super chic on the feminine form.

Make sure your socks are plain and super fine.
No hideous men's gym socks, please.

A man's belt lends an androgynous edge to any style of trousers.

Flat, masculine
shoes add an
Androgyne
element to
any outfit.

A manly hat looks great
above a sleek hairstyle and
neutral make-up.

Jewellery should be minimal. A pair of smart cufflinks is all the glitter that an Androgyne needs.

Your watch should be large, but never flash.

'Think monochrome with a hint of sparkle.'

A plain navy or black tie looks terrific with a crisply tailored white shirt.

Keep make-up simple with neutral
colours and a rose balm for lips
and cheeks.

'Dare to wear men's cologne.'

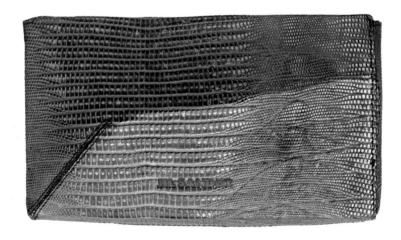

Carry a simple, plain-coloured bag in leather.

'2 Man', a scent by
Comme des Garçons.

Androgyne beauty

Androgyne beauty is strong, honed and sleek. Whoa! We know what you're thinking, 'Great. I don't have to do my hair or wear any make-up.' Do you think that Marlene Dietrich ever stepped out of her limo with a shiny forehead and spots? You bet your silk cravat she did not. Lee Miller braved World War II combat zones with her camera on her shoulder and her hair always immaculately coiffed. The Androgyne cultivates a masculine look with a polished feminine twist. It's a look that says, 'I know where my real beauty lies and I don't have to add any frills or gloss to show it off.' It's a look that requires skill and confidence.

Your hair may be long or short, but it will be sleek. Invest in a good hair cream that will hold your hair in place without making it look wet.

Keep your make-up practically free from colour. Eyes should be very clean with a slight greyish colour on the eyelid and then just a flash of mascara. Brows are arched and dramatically defined, almost slightly too dark for your colouring. Make them clean and strong (think Nastassja Kinski), but not overly heavy (Gus the Gorilla).

Rather than flush the front of your cheeks with a rosy glow, use blusher in a natural shade to sculpt and bring out the contours of your cheekbones. Keep your lips very nude and matt. The look is strong at the top of your face, gradually disappearing into almost nothing.

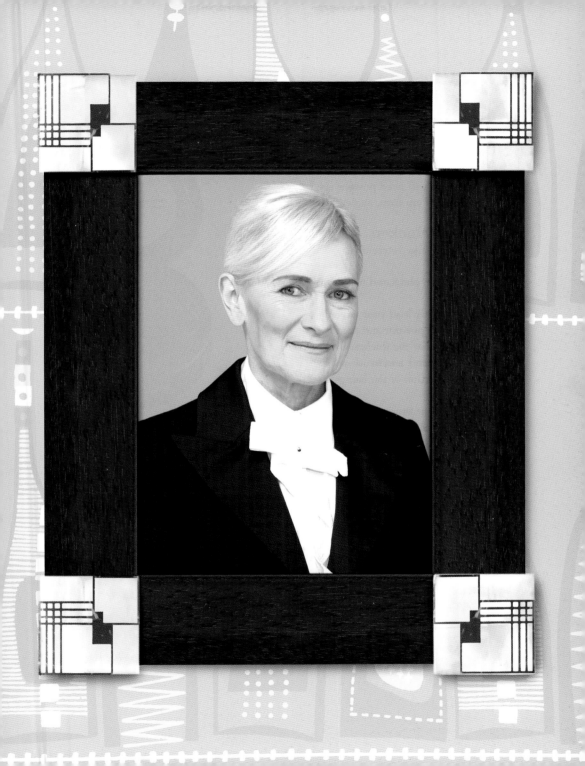

How to do the Androgyne look

Shaping your brows

To shape
You will need powder shadow and a 1/2 cm firm, angled brow brush.

To thicken
A chalky retractable pencil.

First, pluck and neaten your brow line.

Lightly load your angled brow brush with powder and tap off excess. Start at the thickest part of your eyebrow and brush outward in the direction of the hair growth.

If your brows are sparse, use a chalky pencil to thicken the natural line.

Set it all in place with a brow gel.

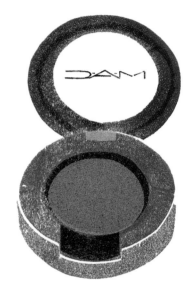

Angled brow brush.

Chalky retractable pencil.

Tip: 'To set unruly brows for the day we love Shavata eyebrow gel.'

A quiff

Slick the sides of your hair back with a little hair cream. If it is long enough, tie it in a low ponytail so that from the front it looks like short hair.

Section off a piece at the front as if it were thick fringe. Back comb the fringe in sections. Take the whole fringe section, push it forward and then twist and pin the tail of it down into a little quiff, using crossed Kirby grips.

ICE QUEEN

YOU'RE ENIGMATIC, COOL PERFECTION

So you want to be an Ice Queen today?

Ice Queen — *'Reserve, formality, coldness of manner', 'a presiding Goddess', 'a woman that is pre-eminent in excellence, beauty, etc'.*
CHAMBER'S DICTIONARY

She's still got it. Still has that air of mystery about her, even though she died more than twenty-five years ago, and her tragic end had to happen under less than clear circumstances. During her lifetime she appeared as untouchable as a crystal sculpture. We are, of course, talking about the serene Grace Kelly. There can't be a woman on earth who has not at some point wished for a piece of her fairytale life, her beauty, her composure, and her wardrobe.

So, let's say today is one of those times. You want a porcelain-smooth exterior that contradicts the burning furnace lying beneath this icy façade. There is nothing sexier than a woman who needs melting and you rather relish the idea of your existing or potential partner having to work hard to attract your attention. It would be enthralling to disguise your inner passion behind a composed twin set and pearls, to captivate with perfection.

Thing is, you don't even vaguely resemble Her Serene Highness, The Princess of Monaco. Your hair is a deep chestnut and you've broken out in a bad case of spots. There is, you feel, nothing graceful about you. The mirror's reflection tells you that you are a little on the chunky side. And untouchable...well, that's a joke, too. Let's nip this negativity in the bud. By all accounts, Grace Kelly was less than frigid below the surface. Do we know for sure what went on behind all that clever studio lighting and under those voluminous skirts? That's the point of the Ice Queen style — it's a veneer, a façade of perfection, masking, we hope, some proper wickedness.

Spots and unruly hair are easily dealt with. Hairspray and a simple application of concealer will do the trick. Swapping sloppy, unwashed clothes for a more tailored, nipped-in silhouette will make you feel clean and virginal. The combination of a trim and tidy outfit and a charming demeanour will inspire admiration, too. Minimise jewellery: pearls for the day, diamonds at night. Swap your woolly mittens for leather gloves (better for shaking hands), exchange boots for court shoes. Jeans…well, they must be relegated to the darkest corner of your wardrobe along with your iPod. To get into the mood, listen to a Doris Day record while sipping your Earl Grey from a bone china cup. If any noisy youths pass by your window with their boom boxes, throw them a regally disdainful glance. Later, settle onto the sofa to watch *Marni* by Alfred Hitchcock, starring that exemplary Ice Queen, Tippi Hedren.

Observe other Ice Queens, such as Rosamund Pike and Nicole Kidman. One of their common attributes is innate politeness and good manners. All Ice Queens must treat others with respect. Gagging your swear words will instantly make you seem more ladylike. Saying a gracious 'Good morning' to neighbours, road sweepers and parking wardens is a really nice thing to do. Kind actions make you feel good. Doing your little bit for charity will bolster self-esteem. Give and you will receive.

Carry off Ice Queen like you mean it and you will surely be worshipped from afar.

Ice Queen wardrobe essentials

Clothes

- PASTEL SKIRT SUITS
- TWIN SETS
- SILK COCKTAIL DRESSES
- PUSSY-BOW BLOUSES
- FITTED SHIFT DRESSES
- CRISP, WHITE SHIRTS
- CASHMERE CARDIGANS

Colour, pattern and texture

- GREYS, SILVER AND WHITE
- LACE
- FUR TRIM
- KID LEATHER
- TWEED

Take design inspiration from

- PRADA
- BURBERRY PRORSUM
- MULBERRY
- VALENTINO
- AQUASCUTUM

Daytime Ice Queen

The Ice Queen look is ultimately regal. Your clothes are conservative in the extreme, but that doesn't mean frumpy. You are a princess, not a librarian. As an Ice Queen you project a definite air of 'look, don't touch'. If your neckline is too low or your skirt is too short, you are missing the mark.

How to not look frumpy

Your knits must be fitted to your body, and never be square or baggy. Your colours are pale and blended, but not drab. Your accessories look expensively understated. Tights are sheer and nude, never black. Skirts skim your silhouette without being overly short or tight. Your hemline always stops at the crease of your knee. Make the most of your ankles and legs by playing up their elegance with simple court shoes.

Colour

Ice Queen tones are always at the paler end of the palette – muted, not bright. Your outfits never jar with clashing colours. The Ice Queen is a suit lover, so you often wear all one colour. Blend separates beautifully by wearing the same hue in different shades. Virginal white is the staple of the Ice Queen wardrobe. Everyone suits one shade of white. Yours might be ice white, ivory or cream.

Texture

You look as though you would be luxurious to the touch – if you ever allowed anyone to get close enough. You love soft satins and silks and mix them with heavier tweeds and fine knits.

Knits

The texture of your knits is key. Cashmere and fine merino convey expensive perfection. Avoid furry angora or mohair – they're far too cute and little girly. It goes without saying that you would not be seen dead in a fisherman's sweater or other chunky knit. Even if you have very big boobs you wear a demurely high neckline, so jumpers must be plain. A twin set is great for instantly creating an Ice Queen look. The modern Ice Queen always wears it fitted at the waist.

'It's as much
about poise
as the clothes
you wear.'

'Choose evening
fabrics that
shimmer rather
than sparkle.'

Night-time Ice Queen

An Ice Queen really shines at night, not by piling on the glitter and rhinestones but rather by outclassing every other woman in the room.

Texture and colour

Glamour is conveyed by the way you shimmer. Heavy silk fabrics or soft metallic threads help to give the aura of a heavenly body that just wafted down the staircase. Remember to keep colours soft and pale.

Jewellery

All your jewellery looks like it has been passed down through generations of Ice Queens. You don't wear modern pieces. The Ice Queen look is expensive, simple and understated. A pair of diamond studs (or cubic zirconium – who knows the difference?) or a strand of pearls will suffice. Necklaces never dangle or clank. Your watch is delicate. Brooches in different stones are the icing on your coats and jackets. A brooch is very regal and you, after all, are an Ice Queen.

Dresses

The colour palette of Trinny's dress on page 95 defines her as an Ice Queen. You have no call to fall back onto black. Whether it has a pencil skirt or an A-line, an Ice Queen dress is always fitted in the bodice. Your dress frames your face without fighting with your features. You do not deign to expose your cleavage, but you may choose to play up your décolletage in a strapless dress with a bare graceful neck or a simple string of pearls. There's no need for flashy diamonds around the neck. Wear your dress with sheer natural tights or no tights at all.

Shoes

Shoes are understated and, like your outfit, complement your skin tone. They are never an item to be admired in their own right. Their purpose is to extend your legs and lend the most elegant shape to your lower leg and ankle. On page 95, Susannah wears a slimmer heel to flatter her slim ankles, while Trinny's heel is thicker to make her sturdier ankles appear svelte.

Ice Queen finishing touches

Ice Queen accessories are nothing other than discreet punctuation marks to your clean, tailored look. Everything is immaculate and it all blends in a sleek hum of polished perfection.

A slim belt looks great over a fitted jumper. Your belts serve to add neatness to your waist, rather than make a statement.

Ice Queen shoes are classic courts. Your heels are elegant, but not too high.

Kid gloves are the perfect accessory.

Your handbag always blends
with your outfit.

Your jewellery is small and understated,
yet of unmistakeable quality.

Nothing says 'Ice Queen' more
perfectly than a strand of pearls.

'An Ice Queen is polished
and untouchably perfect.'

Ice Queen make-up is unobtrusive.

Wear nothing but Chanel No. 5.

Ice Queen beauty

Whether she is on her way to the supermarket or Buckingham Palace, an Ice Queen faces the world with a cool mask of perfection. The essence of Ice Queen make-up is pale and soft. Your look begins with the kind of flawless foundation that a marble statue of Venus would be proud of.

Groom your brows and shape them with a brow powder that exactly matches your colouring. Choose tones of matt grey eyeshadow and blend, blend, blend. Enhance your eyes with a couple of subtle false lashes, applied just in the outer corners.

Your cheeks will have a hint of colour to match lips that are finished in cool, blueish pink with a soft sheen. An Ice Queen never wears gloss or frosted lipstick. And no kissing is allowed.

Finish the look of Princess perfection with manicured, baby pink nails.

An Ice Queen just doesn't have a 'bad hair day'. Your roots are done and your hair is swept up into an unmoveable, 'don't touch' pleat or bun. Keep a small can of hairspray in your handbag. If it's windy or raining outside, simply cancel lunch and stay at home.

How to do the Ice Queen look

Flawless skin

For dry or normal skin: using a primer will fix your face in place for the day with minimal need for powder. For oily or combination skin: choose an oil-free primer that will keep your skin matt as well as give a great base.

Apply foundation with fingers.

Use sparingly and build up layers where needed.

Only use on parts of your face where it's needed, and blend out well.

Don't put foundation under your eyes (you will use concealer there).

Make sure that your under-eye concealer matches your skin tone. Dab it from the innermost corner of your eye outwards and then blend it with a brush.

Spots or scarring should be covered with a separate concealer using a cotton bud or clean brush.

Only use powder if your face is still shiny at the end of the process. Use a loose powder and dust it on with a brush.

French pleat

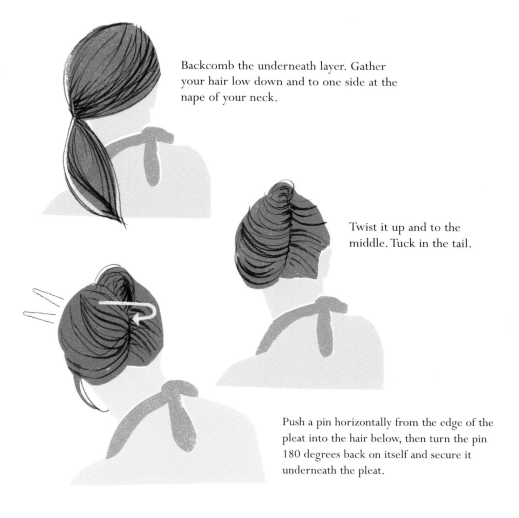

Backcomb the underneath layer. Gather your hair low down and to one side at the nape of your neck.

Twist it up and to the middle. Tuck in the tail.

Push a pin horizontally from the edge of the pleat into the hair below, then turn the pin 180 degrees back on itself and secure it underneath the pleat.

AVANT-GARDE ECCENTRIC

You're an individual intellectual

So you want to be an
Avant-Garde Eccentric today?

Avant-Garde Eccentric — 'Unusual or experimental' and 'unconventional and slightly strange'.

OXFORD ENGLISH DICTIONARY

The world has become so homogenised. Bureaucracy rules our lives with impending identity cards, CCTV and even a census on our sex lives. Blandness is rife. Everyone is slavishly following fashion because they don't have the imagination to sail off-course. Women have identikit boob jobs, blown-up lips, bum implants, cheek/wrinkle/nose fillers. There are waiting lists for the one style of bag. You just want to SCREAM at the similarity of it all. 'Arrrgh! Let me OUT of here!' You're strangled by sameness. The frustration of having to conform to be accepted is driving you mad. It has got to the point where you are ready to plead insanity to break free from the red tape that herds us together. You yearn to be different and long to be liberated from ready-made meals and shopping malls.

Avant-Garde Eccentric is a bold style. A little madness is required, backed up by a fierce individualism that wages war against a congealed high street. But does it feel far too 'out there' for your conventional life? What will the neighbours think? There are no resources for a distinctive dresser because high street shops sell more or less the same stuff. Oh, and you are far too shy. And yet that little psychedelic monkey continues to whisper words of revolution in your ear. We know you want to rebel. It is surprisingly easy to mix up the norm, turning everyday clothing into Avant-Garde Eccentric style. You must unburden yourself of established images. Look at Isabella Blow. What a wonderful example of someone who dared to be different in spite of her shyness and insecurity. She celebrated her unusual looks with flair and drama, as did and do scions of Avant-Garde Eccentric style, Diana Vreeland and Anna Piaggi. These women inspire fashion rather than conform to it.

To get in the mood, rent a few 1920s Dadaist films. Dance in the park in your bare feet. Shuffle your wardrobe. Mix and don't match. Add theatrics with hats and bright lips. Boas, scarves and paste jewellery made by your kids work fabulously when worn all together. Become a bit lesbian in your manner… smoke a cigar and drink whisky. Put down Joanna Trollope and read romantic poetry. Talking to yourself in the car makes you feel really wacky, a bit like running down the street naked, but not as extreme.

And the point of all this lunacy? It's so damn invigorating. You will feel alive, alert, interesting. Your shyness will evaporate when you notice strangers being drawn to your startling presence. While on the one hand you will stand out like a beacon, you can also hide behind your wild attire. Your clothes will be the talking point. Consider yourself a walking work of art. You will be analysed and scrutinised. Some might think you have gone too far, but they will be the me-too conformists wearing cropped pants and driving a Volvo. The one thing you will never be considered is boring.

Rise up against Ms Average and stand fast in something wild and fanciful so as never to be forgotten.

You are not a number, you are a free woman.

Avant-Garde Eccentric wardrobe essentials

Clothes

- PALAZZO PANTS
- COWL-NECK SWEATERS
- LONG COATS
- LONG SKIRTS
- KAFTANS
- FAKE FUR JACKET
- NEPALESE COAT

Colour, pattern and texture

- HUGE FLORAL PRINTS
- BEADING
- FEATHER TRIM
- LAYERING
- NET

Take design inspiration from

- DRIES VAN NOTEN
- PHILIP TREACY
- CHRISTIAN LACROIX
- ALBERTA FERRETTI
- VERA WANG

Daytime Avant-Garde Eccentric

At first, it takes much courage to wear the Avant-Garde Eccentric look during the day. No cover of darkness, no chance of pretending that you're just off to a charity fancy dress ball. Once you have conquered your fear and indulged in the pure, glorious fun of stepping out dressed like a human peacock we are sure that you will find it addictive.

Hats

A great way to dip your toe in the water is to get hold of an amazing, fabulous hat. We're not talking about a classic fedora or stetson or beret. We're talking about a piece of sculpture that sits on top of your head. The best bear the names of Philip Treacy or Stephen Jones, but a search on eBay should always return a few great candidates. To be sure of success, keep the rest of your outfit architectural and simple. It's the plinth for your milliner's work of art. If you really embrace this look you could go to the extreme of someone with the flair of Isabella Blow – mixing so many wild elements that your hat becomes just a bird in the forest.

Print and texture

Your look encompasses an excess of embroidery, beading and appliqué. You're not frightened to layer rough with smooth textures or to wear prints and mix them up. Prints should be bold, you're seldom seen in a cute sprig design. Colours are always rich. Imagine a beautiful Chinoiserie dress with a fuchsia coat, an incredible tapestry bag and a stack of amazing jewelled bangles clanking up one dramatic arm.

Piling it on

Avant-Garde Eccentric dressing is invariably BIG dressing. Wearing one fabulous ring is stylish, wearing three is a really making a grand statement. Everything that you wear has its own story. Your outfit is not fashion. It's a form of self-expression that says, 'I'm not afraid to be seen.' Be prepared to take risks. You can't get it right without occasionally getting it wrong.

'Your outfit is
not fashion.
It's a form of
self-expression.'

'Every piece you
wear is a unique
show stopper.'

Night-time Avant-Garde Eccentric

Your outfit is an expression of the full extent of your imagination, but you are not in fancy dress. An Avant-Garde Eccentric is truly happy at an art gallery opening or a poetry reading – surrounded by the people who will really appreciate what she wears.

Vintage

Avant-Garde Eccentric dressing is about totally unique pieces. These are the foundations of your outfit. You pick up garments from diverse sources: markets, antique shops and travels abroad, so there is no chance of taking direction from fashion magazines or shop window mannequins. Train your eye and learn to think for yourself. This isn't about recreating a bygone era. It's about wearing antique pieces in contemporary ways. You might choose a 1950s dress, but by the time you've put it together with an embroidered coat and an African beaded belt your audience (you always have an audience) hardly knows from when or where it has come.

We don't believe you have to be born with this skill, but we do believe that it requires a bit of study. Look at Avant-Garde Eccentric icons like Daphne Guinness, Diana Vreeland, Björk and Josephine Baker. Go to a vintage shop and let your eye wander until it is inexorably drawn to a fabulous print, a rich fabric or a piece of embroidery. Try it on and ask yourself, 'What can I do to make this work?' Maybe the neckline needs to be re-cut to suit your body shape or perhaps it's simply a matter of adding contemporary tights and shoes.

Box of inspiration

The Avant-Garde Eccentric look could soon take over your wardrobe, your house and your life. Unless you aspire to becoming a full-time Avant-Garde Eccentric, keep a collection of bits and pieces that you have acquired in your travels in a box or drawer, to be brought out on days when you would like to be inspired.

Avant-Garde Eccentric finishing touches

What is the secret to Avant-Garde Eccentric accessorising? It's no secret — pile it on! The Avant-Garde Eccentric is incapable of being discreet. We can see you coming from next Christmas.

The number of bangles you wear is limited only by how long your arms are.

An Avant-Garde Eccentric has a handbag for every occasion. Your bag is not practical, it's a part of your ensemble.

Jewellery can be from any and every era or culture. Just make sure that it is big and plentiful.

A fabulous, stand-alone hat is the pinnacle of every Avant-Garde Eccentric outfit.

Choose shoes in rich materials and exquisite colours.

RANJAN
Body Decor

Supplement your
make-up with
bindis or
rhinestones.

You're not
afraid to add
strongly coloured
lipstick to your
look.

Avant-Garde Eccentric make-up
is not designed merely to enhance
your features, it makes a
statement in its own right.

'Your
make-up
accessories
are pure
body art.'

'Arpège', a scent by Lanvin.

Avant-Garde Eccentric beauty

An Avant-Garde Eccentric looks simply amazing at all times. Your clothes are a creation and your hair and make-up are works of art in their own right. This is definitely the most fun you are ever going to have with make-up, so really go to town.

In magpie fashion, start collecting fabulous bits and pieces to keep in your make-up box: glitters, rhinestones, wild eyelashes and vibrantly coloured eyeshadows and lipsticks. It's probably worth practising in front of the mirror on the day before you decide to do the full Avant-Garde Eccentric look. Choose precious stone colours that will complement your outfit and then be adventurous. You might want to add glittery bindis to the corners of your eyes to elongate your eye line. Or stick rhinestones along your cheekbone with eyelash glue. Or maybe indulge in a pair of those extravagant, feathered false eyelashes. Most make-up rules tell you to emphasise the eyes or the lips, but not both. The Avant-Garde Eccentric respects no such rules. You happily add a berry or fuchsia lip stain and get away with it.

Whichever hairstyle you choose, it will always be extreme. It might be slicked back with a twist, piled high, or short and flat on top. It might be big and wild, it might be coloured bright red or blonde with black stripes or decorated with birds or silk flowers or topped with a little hat. It will never be timid or boring. So make sure that you leave enough time in the morning to work on your hair. Big, wide hair looks great with a dramatic outfit and it's simple to do:

1. Tong your hair with small tongs using plenty of hairspray on each strand.

2. Pull out each strand with your fingers, separating it all to create fullness.

3. Massage your roots underneath with your fingers, and apply lots and lots of hairspray.

How to do the Avant-Garde Eccentric look

Your box of tricks

Rhinestones.

Glitter liner.

Lash Pearls by Givenchy.

Tip: 'Use glitter liner in conjunction with bindis and lash pearls.'

Tip: 'Use fancy false lashes with feathers or in bright colours on their own for a more dramatic effect or try using brightly coloured eyeshadows with bindis in complementary, not contrasting, colours.'

Fancy false eyelashes.

Bindis.

Bright, peacock eyeshadow set.

Diva

You're sultry and sexy

So you want be a Diva today?

Diva — '*From the Latin* diva, *Goddess*'.

OXFORD ENGLISH DICTIONARY

A new day dawns — you feel DIVINE. You are emotionally strong and ruler of all you survey. Your home feels like your kingdom, your taxi becomes a chauffeur-driven Bentley. Your mood must be matched by an outer precision that needs to be perfect. You are aware this takes time, but that's not a problem because, heavens, you don't care if you are a bit, or even a lot, late. Any inconvenience caused will be swept aside with a husky 'daaarrling' and your most disarming smile.

Are you feeling a little Diva-ish? You bet! Take advantage of this potent mood to get things done…yesterday.

Arrrgh! Can you pull it off? Can you maintain divinity for a whole day? You have to fit in a trip to IKEA and your only clean clothes are your trusty jeans. And it's *Match of the Day*. Try as you might, it's impossible to visualise Lana Turner munching on pizza while wearing a Man U home shirt. Also, you're just too much of a pussycat to render your builder into a submissive, panting mess with one withering gaze. Flawlessness is threatening and you are not, but isn't that the idea? You are not here to make friends today — you want to achieve world domination through your heavenly aura. You can swat enemies like flies and blow smoke into the eyes of those who dare cross you. Just be sure that the cigarette is clamped into an elegant holder.

This demanding goddess holds no prisoners. 'No' is not a word recognised in her vocabulary. She is a woman of extremes who would rather buy General Electric than change the light bulb herself. She doesn't pout to get her own way like the Bombshell. No, she smoulders people into submission. Men are intimidated by the Diva. She is beyond reach, beyond reproach, eternal. Her image is unequivocal. Think of Elizabeth Taylor, Rita Hayworth and Ava Gardner. The motivation of a Diva is to be adored. Worshipped would be ideal, like Cleopatra and Sophia Loren. Contemporary Diva, Dita von Teese, comes close as she blends an untouchable grace with the fact that her day job involves getting her kit off in front of an audience.

The common bond between these Divas is that their worlds were and are a shrine to them. Their wishes were others' commands. They could have led armies willingly to a sure death or astronauts to other worlds. All you're asking for is a leaking tap to be fixed. Put on a Shirley Bassey CD and get into the flow. As the lady says, 'Diamonds are Forever.' Assuming a super-glamorous persona will make the earth move for you.

Things will happen.

001

ERA HOUSE
GARDEN
opolis Music pres

LA TRAVIATA

smoking building   Auditorium

Diva wardrobe essentials

Clothes

- FITTED EVENING GOWNS WITH TRAIN
- FISHTAIL PENCIL SKIRTS
- FUR COATS
- FITTED SUITS
- SILK SHIRTS

Colour, pattern and texture

- ANIMAL PRINTS
- RICH, DEEP COLOURS
- JEWEL TRIM
- ORGANDIE
- BLACK SATIN
- RED AND BLACK
- RUCHING
- CHINESE EMBROIDERY

Take design inspiration from

- ALEXANDER MCQUEEN
- ELIE SAAB
- JOHN GALLIANO
- LOUIS VUITTON
- CHRISTIAN DIOR

Daytime Diva

A Diva must always be prepared to meet her public and sign a few autographs. Even in daylight hours, you go out impeccably attired in clothes that most of us would only dare to don for a super-smart evening event or the theatre. To you, the sports-wear department is an alien planet. A Diva simply does not own a pair of jeans, let alone trainers!

Blouse
Drama is your watchword. Look out for blouses with incredible sleeves and fabulous collars. Pearl or jet buttons are perfectly acceptable for Diva day wear, as are silk, satin or organdie shirts. Vintage stores are a rich source of great blouses. Steer clear of M&S or the boring 'business blouse'.

Coat
Your coat needs to maintain the same strength and flair as the rest of your look. Your classic coats feature feminine tailoring, either deeply waisted or dramatically flared. The fabric could be a show-stopping animal print or satin. A pea coat or man's car coat would be far too prosaic.

Fabrics
Your fabrics are luxurious and always have an evening edge. The colours are rich and the print is extravagant. A Diva would not be seen dead in denim, tweed or gingham. You may well wear a satin dress to lunch or a pair of crepe trousers for a stroll in the park (with black sunglasses, naturally).

Shoes
Casual shoes are for casual folk. A Diva wears only heels.

'A Diva looks
more at
home on the
red carpet
than at the
supermarket.'

'You are the
star of your
own show.'

Night-time Diva

Darkness is a Diva's natural habitat. You are most at home in an opera house. Every millimetre of your night-time outfit works to play up your femininity, but without the overt flirtatiousness of the Bombshell. While the Bombshell's look says, 'Come on, have a go' and the Ice Queen's veneer says, 'You may look, but do not touch', your Diva look conveys the message, 'Only approach if you are brave enough.' Take inspiration from glamorous 1940s film stars.

Long gown

Every Diva's wardrobe contains at least one full-length glamour gown. You are always ready to be invited to the Oscars. The colour will be dramatic and the shape will make your waist look wonderful. Your dress is made to frame your shape and always has a strong silhouette. It is never broken up by frills or ruffles.

Cocktail dress

The Diva doesn't do the cute Little Black Dress look. Your cocktail dress is tailored. The skirt may be bum-hugging or dramatically flared, but your bodice is always fitted and affords a fine view of your décolletage.

Corseting

Diva is always clever at creating a studied shape. The wasp waist required for ultimate Diva dressing relies on corseting. Corseting can be worn as a foundation garment or as part of your outer dress.

Shoes

Diva shoes are vertiginously high to give the impression that you never walk any distance greater than from limo door to red carpet. You prefer a round toe and some form of added embellishment – beading, crystals, feathers or print.

Diva finishing touches

Sweet simplicity is not the Diva way. Your divineness demands to be swathed in jewels and furs at every hour of the day. If you do deign to emerge during daylight, make sure that you always have a pair of the very darkest dark glasses to hand.

If you must smoke, do so with dramatic emphasis.

Divas wear heels, even around the house. Your shoes are round-toed or peep-toed and you love a bit of added texture, feather, animal print or rhinestone.

Great corsetry is the foundation of the Diva silhouette.

While most people would wear a luxurious wrap only to the opera or a red carpet event, a Diva dons a wrap for a trip to the newsagent.

What to do when overcome by your own brilliance? Sit down for a moment and fan yourself.

Diva make-up should be dark and
dramatic, like everything else about you.

Make sure that your jewellery is
big and sparkly, and can be seen
from the back of the concert hall,
if not the moon.

'Pearls de Lalique',
a scent by Lalique Parfums.

'Cleopatra would
envy your jewels.'

A Diva's hand just begs to be kissed
and should sport a knockout gem.

Diva beauty

A Diva is a demanding, divine goddess. Your presentation is polished, sultry and sexy on the dark side. A single glance from beneath your arched brow and lowered lashes will instantly get red ropes pulled back and upgrades offered.

The Diva look has its perfectly dyed roots in the 1940s. Start with a full base – primer, foundation and concealer. Finish your face with a dusting of loose powder if needed – it's most important that the Diva visage does not crack or shine.

Use brow powder and pencil to make your eyebrows strong and quite dark (see page 92 in the Androgyne chapter for instructions on how to achieve this). Contrast your brows with clean, light eyeshadow and create a cat-like sweep with liquid liner and long lashes.

Keep colours deep and dramatic: use a berry stain for your lips, a plummy blusher under your cheekbones and a dark burgundy nail varnish.

You are often to be seen in strapless gowns, so lavish attention on your décolletage. Exfoliate and moisturise your neck and chest, and for super-glamorous occasions, use a bust-enhancing mask before sallying forth.

Your coiffure (we can confidently call it that) is a classic style and deeply glamorous. There is not a hair out of place as you sweep down the marble staircase, never so much as glancing at the men falling like nine-pins in your wake.

How to do the Diva look

Cat's eyes

Cream eye base: Use a shade lighter than your skin tone. Rub it on lightly, using your finger to even out.

Liquid eyeliner: Sit down and steady your elbow on a table. Close your eye, follow the natural line of your eyelid from the innermost corner to the outermost. Then, with your eye open, sweep outwards to lift the natural corner of your eye.

Eyelash curler: Clamp and hold at the base of your upper eyelashes for 10 seconds.

Mascara: Press mascara wand into the root of your eyelashes and hold. Let the base coat dry, then apply one or two full coats, sweeping from the root to the tip of the top lashes only.

False lashes: Stick long, individual lashes into the outer third of your eyelid.

The Diva wave

Use medium tongs. Start by holding the open tong at ear level, no higher than that. Take a section of hair, spray it, and wind it around the tong (not the tong around the hair), winding it towards your head and all in the same direction, working from the front towards the back of your head. Do the other side the opposite way so that it meets in the middle. Do NOT close the tongs (that will create an ugly kink in your hair). Simply use the open tong like a hot stick.

Once you have tonged both sides, separate your hair with a large-tooth comb. The hair will create a wave that flows around your head. Set it into place with hairspray.

SOPHISTICATE
YOU'RE ASSURED AND STYLISH

So you want to be a Sophisticate today?

A sophisticated person — *'showing worldly experience and knowledge of fashion and culture'*.

OXFORD ENGLISH DICTIONARY

Oh, to be organised. Oh, to be anal...just once. How wonderful to look perennially pulled together as opposed to pulled apart. To have a home that was tidy for once. Think of all those lovely houses in *Architectural Digest*. White everything, with sheets ironed twice — once on the board and then again on the bed. This is a world without stains or creases. Here there is a dining table eternally laid and ready to welcome a list of super-chic friends. In this world, dogs don't do-do and children eat all their greens. This world doesn't allow for human error or erratic behaviour. This world is safe in its order. Oh, the glory of sophistication.

Is it possible that sophistication can be acquired overnight? Doesn't it take years of highbrow stimulation, high-flying jobs and penthouse living? Isn't it something born from decades of self-discipline? You have led a life of ordered-in pizza, dancing on tables and *Sex and the City*. How on earth can you capture the rather sinister poise of an Anna Wintour? Surely her life must be about containment on every count? Does she do anything fun, anything spontaneous? Don't these refined beings make a date for sex like they do a business meeting? This is just not YOU!

A Sophisticate does project a certain coolness, but this may be better seen as composure and self control. Sophistication is a protective veneer, highly polished, but a veneer all the same. We don't for one second imagine that Wallis Simpson caught the future king with her looks. It was her self-assured, confident personality that took custody of our monarch. To get the balance just right, study Meryl Streep's masterful portrayal of a Sophisticate magazine editor in *The Devil Wears Prada*. Try silence for size. A Sophisticate doesn't feel the need to gabble constantly. For the Sophisticate, less is more on every count. De-cluttering your life — house, wardrobe and desk — is an immensely cathartic process. Before you leave home for the day, take off one thing that you are wearing. Organise your wardrobe into summer and winter sections. Be chic and simply dressed, with a slight air of haughtiness. Take the time to handwrite letters instead of emailing, and swap your pansies for an orchid that you re-position three times a day.

Why do you think a sophisticated woman is more successful than, let's say, the Boho chick. It's because, yes, she wants to be; but it's also because she has given herself the freedom to focus on what is important to her. By emptying her world of surplus clutter, she can clearly see her goals. When you dress like you are in control, with precision and style, you will be amazed to see how readily other people treat you with respect, how easily doors open and new opportunities arise. If you are feeling a little lost or that you are not being heard, harden your resolve, put on the armour and kick some arse – with a fine leather court shoe, of course.

The Sophisticate ALWAYS gets what she wants.

M
Newsm

Dorothy Wilding

WOMAN OF THE YEAR   Number 1

ishop of Canterbury: "Truly this has been wonderful."
(See FOREIGN NEWS)

no-obligation design consultation.

Sophisticate wardrobe essentials

Clothes

◆ TAILORED SUITS
◆ FLOWING, WIDE-LEG TROUSERS
◆ FITTED SHIRTS
◆ A-LINE SKIRTS
◆ WOOL DRESSES

Colour, pattern and texture

◆ TWEED
◆ GOLD BUTTONS
◆ NAVY
◆ PLEATS
◆ SILK CREPE
◆ PLAIN COLOURS
◆ BLACK AND WHITE

Take design inspiration from

◆ CHANEL
◆ BALENCIAGA
◆ OSCAR DE LA RENTA
◆ ALLEGRA HICKS
◆ PRADA

Daytime Sophisticate

If you are in your mid-40s onwards and you want to exude a clean, confident look, try grown-up Sophisticate rather than girly Gamine and you will never look like mutton dressed as lamb. The mark of a Sophisticate is her classically timeless way of dressing. We wouldn't know if you bought your suit or trousers last week or in 1946.

White shirt

A classic white shirt is one of the staples in a Sophisticate wardrobe. You know better than anyone how to dress it up or down. If you wear jeans, for example, it is never with a t-shirt but rather with a crisp, well-cut white shirt. The body should be fitted, with any volume or embellishment confined to the sleeves.

Jackets

The Sophisticate is definitely a jacket wearer. You understand smart separates better than anyone. Whether your jacket has a princess collar or a V neck, it is fitted at the waist with a neat shoulder, never a large shoulder pad. Your jacket is integral to completing your look – not just something slung on to keep you warm.

Trousers

You wear a lot of trousers, always tailored in classic fabrics like wool gaberdine. Avoid the ultra-trendy leg shape or fashionable waistband. Your trousers are beautiful classics that will last for decades.

Jewellery

A Sophisticate rarely wears stand-out jewellery, with the notable exception of the chain belt – a favourite since Sophisticate icon Coco Chanel made it synonymous with chic dressing. Otherwise your jewellery is confined to a delicate pair of drop earrings, a wedding band and a functional, yet chic, watch. Occasionally you might veer into wearing a long, elegant necklace that looks like it is a part of your top. On those days, you ditch the earrings and the chain belt.

'The
Sophisticate
look exudes
understated
authority.'

'Classic is your watchword.'

Night-time Sophisticate

Your evening look is understated. You are perfectly presented without needing recourse to big, loud prints or dramatically plunging dresses. A Sophisticate's outfit never shouts, 'Look at me,' yet our eye is always drawn to her innate elegance.

Colour

A very definite colour palette enables you to create chic dressing easily – everything goes with everything else. Sophisticate staples are black, white, navy and grey with a shot of red or shocking pink if you feel like some real colour. Prints are rarely worn and are always combined with a solid colour garment (for example, a red print dress with a solid pink coat).

Long skirt

At night, a Sophisticate is more inclined to wear a cocktail dress than full-on evening gown glamour. If long is required, you might try a full-length black skirt with a chain belt and a perfectly tailored white shirt.

Shoes

Sophisticate shoes serve simply as a leg extension – we hardly ever notice their presence. The main function of your shoes is to add elegance to your ankle and height to your silhouette, not to draw attention to feet that have been embellished with rhinestones or feathers. If anyone asks, 'Where did you get those amazing shoes?' you will know you are on the wrong track.

Sophisticate finishing touches

Sophisticate accessories never jar or clash. They simply add polish and élan to your look.

You don't go in for big, flashy jewellery. A simple long rope of crystals or pearls will suffice.

On most people, a silk square could look frumpy. On you, it looks smart and adds a perfect finishing touch to a plain shirt or jacket.

A Sophisticate always likes to feel in control. Take a tip from Sophisticate icon Anna Wintour and veil your emotions behind big, round sunglasses. Make sure they are free from gold decals or rhinestones.

The Sophisticate loves classics — and what could be more classic than a Birkin handbag? Make sure it's in a muted, neutral colour.

Sophisticate shoes are restrained, muted and give an elegant shape to your leg.

'Use scent and make-up simply to enhance timeless sophistication.'

'White Jasmine and Mint Cologne', by Jo Malone.

Your make-up is neutral
and enhances your features.
Always start with an
immaculate base.

As a Sophisticate, you not only
look harmonious, you also create
a harmonious environment all
around you. Burn scented candles
at home and in the office.

Sophisticate beauty

The Sophisticate is always meticulously groomed. You are a lady who knows what you want and exactly how you want it.

Your look is conservative with a small c. You stick to the classic rules of what suits you and are never swayed by fashion. Start with an application of perfect foundation and concealer to provide the canvas for your make-up.

Make sure your brows are tidily plucked, groomed and pencilled in. For this you will need Tweezerman tweezers and really good nail scissors because the trimming is just as important as the plucking. To get a nicely defined arch, use an eyebrow pencil that's soft and powdery so it doesn't look stiff and solid. Lancôme make a good one.

Use eyeshadows in neutral greys, browns or beiges that suit your skin, hair and eye tones. Never, never, wear bright or high-fashion colours. If the colours that you choose happen to be the flavour of the season, you will be wearing them anyway. Apply mascara with a light touch – you want your lashes to appear natural. Do apply a really good concealer under your eyes to make you look bright and awake.

Then blush the apples of your cheeks in a natural tone. Again, avoid experimental colours, shimmer or glitter.

Your lips are unobtrusive, but perfect. Start with a lip liner pencil that exactly matches your nude, non-colour lip colour. Finish with a soft gloss.

Your hairstyle is never flamboyant. It's a take on a classic look – it could be the classic bob or the classic wave. Absolutely always keep a little headscarf about your person in case of rain. The last thing you want is for your hair to be exposed to bad weather.

How to do the Sophisticate look

Natural blusher

Pinky
Best for:
English rose
Dark hair with pale skin

Blush
Best for:
Everyone

Apricot
Best for:
Warm olive
Warm blonde

Take away the tiredness of your day with a natural toned blusher. For oily skin, use a powder blush. For dry skin, use a cream blush. In hot weather, a gel blush is best for all skin types.

Tip: 'To find the apple of your cheeks, smile without opening your mouth. Apply blusher with your finger or a brush, starting at the apple and sweeping gently back and upwards.'

A perfect neat blowdry

If your hair is soft or fine, apply hair-thickening cream for extra body.
Use heat-protecting lotion to make sure that your hair doesn't get damaged.

When your hair is nearly dry, wrap each section around a big round brush and
dry it at the roots to create lift. Then pull the brush through your hair to give
an inward bend at the ends.

Finish with a burst of hairspray to keep the ends from flying away.

Rock Chick

You're wild and strong

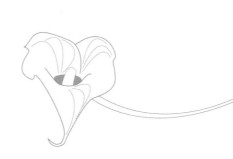

So you want to be a Rock Chick today?

Rock Chick — *'A form of popular music derived from rock and roll but characterised by a more serious approach' and 'a young woman'.*
<small>OXFORD ENGLISH DICTIONARY</small>

You have toed the line all your life. Sheltered childhood, teacher's pet, great grades, daddy's girl. You have played safe, never venturing beyond the proverbial bike shed for a puff on a menthol cigarette. Your job is secure, your mortgage payments up to date and your bank balance hundreds of pounds away from an overdraft. Hey, life is good. Life is secure, your future inevitable. Friends envy your ordered existence and your family are proud of how well they have brought up their little girl. Little do they know how you yearn to swap your glass of Sancerre for a swig of Jack Daniels.

A life of harmony has engendered an inner need for a bout of wild behaviour. You would like permission to swear like a trooper, tell those who annoy you to piss off, leave beds unmade, dishes and hair unwashed, nails chipped. You long to live a day in the life of a Rock Chick. You want to feel dangerous, to drive your friends insane with worry as you live life on the edge. You want to get noticed.

No, you don't need to be a junkie living in a squat à la Nancy Spungen. You can be a Rock Chick without the drugs, but a 24-hour binge of bad behaviour will be a real shot in the arm. Oh, but you can't possibly be so irresponsible. What will the neighbours think? What will Daddy say if you shirk conventionality for a bit? Well, for goodness sake, take a slug of whisky and get on with it. Do you think Debbie Harry ever cared about doing the right thing? Tracey Emin certainly doesn't give a gnat's arse about what other people think of her unruly behaviour. Those girls live to shock.

Rock 'n' roll requires irreverence. Who cares if you sleep late, eat junk food and stay up all night. Being unpredictable keeps people on their toes. A walk

on the wild side will act as a wake-up call for those who take you for granted. Being late, unavailable, un-contactable is no crime once in a while. It's healthy to shake up the household by removing the person that keeps it all together – the sensible, dependable you. When you're done with demonising your spotless reputation, it won't take long to rebuild – everyone will be just so GRATEFUL to have you sane and sound again.

The problem is that there is no way you will seem untamable in pale pink cashmere, holding a crystal glass shimmering in the sunlight that shines through your spotless windows. You must swap the pastels for midnight black. Your hair must look unkempt and messy…more bird's nest than bob. Healthy, fresh make-up must be replaced by porcelain-pale skin and kohl black eyes. No bling for the true Rock Chick, it's chunky silver or nothing. The iron can take a break too, creased clothes exude a sod-it attitude. So throw *The Sound of Music* out the window, you're more of a *Spinal Tap* girl. Crank up the Rock 'n' roll on your car stereo – LOUD – and roll down the windows as you hit the night streets.

Of all the styles we sported in this book, the one we enjoyed putting together most was the Rock Chick. It is a great look to emulate because you really do feel wild and free, and if you are of middling age, like us, a touch of Chrissie Hynde and Marianne Faithfull makes you feel, dare we say it…

Young, hip and cool.

Rock Chick wardrobe essentials

Clothes

- SKINNY JEANS
- MEN'S WHITE SHIRTS
- BLACK WAISTCOATS
- NET SKIRTS
- LOGO T-SHIRTS
- LEATHER JACKETS

Colour, pattern and texture

- SKULL PRINTS
- BLACK AND SILVER
- SEQUINS
- LEATHER
- RIPPED DENIM
- MOHAIR
- BLACK NET

Take design inspiration from

- PAM HOGG
- BELLA FREUD
- ALEXANDER MCQUEEN
- DAY BIRGER ET MIKKELSEN
- LUELLA

Rock Chick

Like the Bombshell and High Maintenance looks, Rock Chick dressing is the embodiment of a way of life. It's a life of late nights and playing hard, a life on the road without tiresome schedules or commitments. Raid your boyfriend's wardrobe and make it your own. It doesn't matter if you are single, what you are projecting is that you're in the throes of a torrid affair and just don't have time go home and get your own clothes or comb your hair.

Colour

There is no colour! It's black, maybe with a bit of silver. If you wore pastel, you would turn to dust.

Oversized square scarf

A big square scarf is both decorative and practical. It's part of the Rock Chick lifestyle. And, of course, it's useful for pulling up over your face when riding shotgun on the back of a motorbike.

Jeans

Your jeans are skin tight, preferably black, and always worn with boots.

Boots

A Rock Chick wears more boots than shoes – and they are all black. Square-toed biker boots, boots with platforms, pointy-toed, spike-heel boots and, for good measure, a pair of thigh-high boots, not made for walking.

T-shirts

If you only have one t-shirt, make sure it features a giant skull or the logo of your favourite rock band. Rips and holes are perfectly acceptable, nay desirable, too.

'Think black!'

'Your LBD
isn't neat or
sophisticated
– it's sexy.'

Rock Chick

Every woman secretly wishes to dress like a Rock Chick.
You just need the *cojones* to do it. Don't be afraid of this look
if you are size 16. Take inspiration from our gorgeous Rock
Chick, Charlotte. There are no rules for day or night, except
these: during the day you look like you've been up all night;
at night you look like you just got out of bed.

Dress
A dress is often layered with a t-shirt or jeans or leggings. Your dress is always
sexy in a ripped and torn way and often features a see-through element, such as
a net skirt or gauzy bodice. Of course it is black, but it's never a Little Black
Dress.

Jewellery
Rock chick jewellery is silver. Reliable motifs include skulls, crucifixes, roses
and daggers — basically anything that you might find featured on a sailor's
tattoo. You can really pile it on and wear earrings with neck chains and rings.

Leggings
Black, cut-off leggings should be ankle length, no shorter. Black tights and
fishnets are also part of your arsenal.

Layering
You never know where you're going to end up next, so layer up. It's a good
idea to wear at least two tops, a jacket, a dress and a pair of leggings or jeans.
By adding and subtracting you can look like you're prepared go out to a club
in London…and then wake up on the beach in Ibiza.

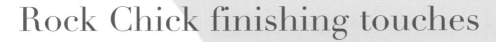

Rock Chick finishing touches

Rock Chick accessories are bad, mean and a little unclean. Silver and black and leather and studs abound.

A skinny black tie will transform any white shirt from office girl to Rock Chick.

Your shoes and boots should be black and kick-ass. Espadrilles or Indian sandals would never darken a Rock Chick's doorstep.

A Rock Chick needs a big scarf. It provides excellent disguise during daylight hours and doubles up as a blanket if you find yourself sleeping on a tour bus.

Ok, so maybe you don't have a big black motorbike – but you do have the gloves.

A studded belt gives attitude to jeans.

A pair of the blackest sunglasses is essential for covering up the fact that you've been up all night and your mascara has run.

ROCK STAR ROCK STAR

Paint your nails the day before and then let them get a bit chipped.

Rock Chick jewellery is always hard-edged. Pile on the skulls and crosses, chains, daggers and silver razor blades.

'A Rock Chick keeps her make-up dark and sultry.'

BAD gal
benefit

LE VERNIS
NAIL COLOUR

461
BLUE SATIN

GIVENCHY

Bumble and bumble.

BLONDISH

HAIR POWDER

poudre beige pour cheveux

NET WT./POIDS NET 4.4 OZ./125 g ℮

'Pure Poison', a scent by Dior.

If your hair is too clean and silky you will never get that grungy, 'just rolled out of bed' look. Mess it up with some dry shampoo.

PURE POISON
Dior
Dior

Rock Chick beauty

This is your chance to go wild in the city, your moment to be thoroughly, wonderfully, reprehensibly baaaaaad. A Rock Chick doesn't care about hair brushes, lip gloss or perfect fingernails. And what better way to stick two fingers up to society than to stand at the bus stop at 8 a.m. looking like you have been partying all night long?

Rock Chick make-up is all about the eyes. Make them almost black using a gun-metal shadow. You can add a bit of glitter, but make sure it is dark and grungy rather than sparkly disco. Your face should be pale with just a touch of shading under your cheekbones to create contour.

Leave your lips nude and quite matt.

For that real 'bedhead', sexy, slept-in look, the trick is to backcomb your hair at the crown with a fine-tooth comb or a tail brush. The more out of condition your hair is, the better this will work. You really want to look like you have slept on the back seat of a tour bus. So you can dry it out and thicken it up with some mousse or styling lotion, rough dry it, take sections and tong it haphazardly. Mix it up. Leave some bits straight and make some bits wavy. If you have flat hair or oily roots, use a powder (Bumble and bumble do a good one) to keep it really dry at the roots. If your roots are growing through, that's all the better.

How to do the Rock Chick look

Smoky eyes

First, use a kohl pencil all over the eyelid.

Then smudge it with a rounded brush.

While the kohl is still wet and sticky, dip a brush into glitter powder and tap off the excess. Pat it on top, working along your eyelid from the inner corner and blending it into the socket.

Run white eyeliner pencil along the inner rim of your lower eyelid.

Finish off with lashings of black mascara.

Messy hair

Thicken up your hair with mousse.

Tong it haphazardly, grab large and small sections and tong in different directions.

Mess it up with your fingers.

MINIMALIST

You're calm and authoritative

So you want to be Minimalist today?

Minimalist — *'Deliberately simple...in design or style'*.
OXFORD ENGLISH DICTIONARY

It's like your world is closing in on you. The clutter in your life is overwhelming. When you rise in the morning, you get out of bed to look down twin barrels of disorder. In your dreams, you lead the life of a Buddhist monk with no call for worldly goods. Your own life is complicated enough without having to decide which necklace goes with that outfit and which shoes go with both. You can't even get into your bedroom, let alone your wardrobe, because of the carnage that is your clothes. Wistfully you think about neatly lined cupboards arranged by uniformity of colour — swathes of calming creams and whites. Wouldn't it feel like heaven to wake up and not have to put together an outfit? Do you long to use clothes as a canvas upon which to print your personality? Today, honey, you must go Minimalist.

The problem is that everything in your wardrobe is flowery or brightly coloured. You have a penchant for frills and live for the next issue of *Heat* magazine. You know that these Minimalist types listen to Philip Glass and Laurie Anderson, but you love the Scissor Sisters. You feel it's impossible to keep things unfussy however much you know that cleanliness is next to godliness.

The Minimalist has no need for fashion magazines but, if you must read them, keep an eye out for women like Anjelica Houston, Tilda Swinton, Sharlene Spiteri and artist Sam Taylor-Wood. They keep their karma with clean lines and unassuming labels. Sam, for one, always heads the best dressed lists, a worthy accolade because she is so unpretentious in her style. It is this subtlety, however, that gets her noticed.

To get into the Minimalist mood, the first thing you must do is have a massive tidy up. It can be superficial — clothes stuffed under the bed — just so long as your office, home or bedroom has an external pristine neatness. It helps if much of your environment is white, so drape a few sheets over those Indian cushions. Orchids give an instant Zen-like atmosphere with their milky perfection. Eating sushi and drinking green tea will cleanse your insides. To clear the mind, swap your nightly schedule of soaps and reality TV for the meditational nothingness of Derek Jarman's film *Blue*. Wearing block colour, sculptural jewellery and a blunt hairstyle will sanitise your outer shell. You could go mad and dye your hair jet black or peroxide blonde, but it's far simpler to reach for a wig. Add a slash of red lipstick, but keep other make-up to a minimum. Did you ever see Charlotte Rampling with drag queen lip liner or Diane Keaton with panda bear eyes? No. These women understand the beauty of a 'nude' face, carefully sculpted with tonal blush and blended concealer.

Minimising the clutter from your world is liberating. You will find you think more clearly and that this clarity of mind will allow you to cull dead wood that is perhaps holding you back. This could be something as simple as clearing your desk, or perhaps gently elbowing out a friend who keeps you down. When one is not swamped by possessions or too many social engagements, there is time and space to appreciate what is truly special in life.

Quality, not quantity, is definitely the motto of the Minimalist.

Minimalist wardrobe essentials

Clothes

- BLACK T-SHIRTS
- BUTTON-UP WHITE SHIRTS
- PALAZZO PANTS
- PUSSY-BOW BLOUSES
- SCULPTURAL DRESSES
- LONG, PLAIN COATS
- ASYMMETRIC SKIRTS

Colour, pattern and texture

- BLOCK COLOURS
- SAME COLOUR WORN ALL OVER
- GRAPHIC PRINTS
- SCULPTURAL FOLDING AND PLEATING
- HIDDEN ZIPS
- ANGLED SEAMS

Take design inspiration from

- ISSEY MIYAKE
- YOHOJI YAMAMOTO
- RICK OWENS
- JIL SANDER
- MARTIN MARGIELA

Daytime Minimalist

The simplest separates are all that is needed for a Minimalist outfit during the day. By keeping the colour uniform and the lines clean, you are half way there. What takes the outfit from neat secretary or therapist to Minimalist is the addition of just one or two strong, sculptural accessories.

Stripping back

Look in the mirror and think not 'What else could I put on?' but rather 'Is there anything that I could take off?' The art of Minimalist dressing is very much about creating a sculptural feel. A Minimalist doesn't believe in soft diaphanous wafts. Your clothing is always quite protective, like a modernist suit of armour.

Textures

You break up your outfit not with pattern but with texture. It's always a modern fabric whether it is sheer, shiny or rough. Details such as cuffs, trim or a print are in same-on-same colour. For example, a white design on a white dress or black leather cuffs on a black gaberdine jacket. Avoid vintage fabrics, such as tapestry, velvet, paisley or lace.

White shirt

A superbly tailored white shirt is one of the key foundations of a Minimalist look. Wear it buttoned up, either with or without a tie.

Coats

A coat is another important item in the Minimalist wardrobe, especially a severe mac, worn tightly belted, not buttoned. A sculptural statement coat is great for evening, perhaps with exaggerated sleeves.

'Create strong
lines and
unexpected
angles.'

'Minimalist
clothes are
based more in
architecture
than in dress-
making.'

Night-time Minimalist

In the evening, don a dramatically sculptural dress. Add one fabulous piece of modern jewellery and those all-important, contemporary, work-of-art shoes. Make sure that your hair and make-up are strong, so as not to soften the look.

Cut

All the great Minimalist dressmakers are master pattern cutters. Look, for example, at the work of Issey Miyake, Yohoji Yamamoto or Azzedine Alaia. Minimalist clothes are feats of engineering rather than dressmaking. Create your dramatic outline with asymmetric seams that give unexpected angles. Look also for interesting shapes created by origami-style pleating and tucking.

Colour

A Minimalist doesn't mix up a lot of colours. Black and white, or navy and black, work well to create a strong Minimalist impression. Equally you might go in for an acid-yellow dress with black shoes.

Belts

A very plain belt can play a supporting role by adding a splash of colour or texture to your plain outfit.

Shoes

Your shoes would be perfectly at home on a plinth at the Tate Gallery. They are strong and sculptural and they stand out against your severe outfit. Heels may be straight, curved or spiked, but you would never go for a cute kitten heel or any kind of bow or fussiness.

Minimalist finishing touches

Minimalism creates beauty by manipulation of space, proportion and material. Being devoid of frills, bows or glitter, Minimalist accessories are, well...minimal. It doesn't mean that there aren't any. It means that each piece is carefully chosen to make a statement. Strong lines and sculptural forms are key.

Make sure that your handbag is unique and beautiful in its simplicity – free from dangly chains or baubles. Don't stuff it too full or you will ruin its pleasing outline.

A piece of Minimalist jewellery is a tactile sculpture in its own right. Whether it's a bold ring, a modern necklace or a huge bangle, it will have the strength to stand alone. Don't mix or pile on your jewellery – set off a single piece against a severe, plain backdrop.

Your shoes present clean, simple lines. They may be a striking colour set against a perfectly plain dress, but they are never beaded or embroidered.

Eve Lom is the Minimalist queen of beauty. This is more than a cleanser, it's a complete beauty routine in a jar.

EVE LOM
CLEANSER / TRAITEMENT DE NETTOYAGE

Your perfect make-up base is merely a backdrop for startling lips. See page 212 for guidance on choosing red lipstick.

'Bois 1920 Vetiver Ambrato', a scent
by Perfumus Firenze.

As a Minimalist, you don't
wear a lot of make-up, but
what there is you apply
with absolute precision.
A high-quality foundation
is essential for this. Your
morning routine might be
as simple as creating a
flawless finish and then
dabbing some Eight Hour
Cream on to your lips.

Minimalist beauty

Don't ever make the mistake of confusing Minimalist make-up with no make-up. Starkly unadorned you are, but fresh and natural you are not. Just as a Zen garden is meticulously raked to create the impression that a perfect wave may have passed over it, so your Minimalist make-up is artfully applied to create the impression of a perfectly blank canvas.

Apply a good base to even out your colouring and use concealer to cover any blemishes. Enhance the shape of your brows with an angled brush and a powder that is very similar to your natural colour. Use an eyebrow pencil to extend the fine ends if necessary.

Then add drama to your face by applying a neutral grey or brown shadow only in the socket creases of your eyelids. Use a browny tone of blusher to add shaping, applying it under your cheekbones rather than onto the apples of the cheeks. Bring it around a little and blend it into the front of your face to avoid creating 'motorway blusher'.

All this is designed to spotlight the main exhibit: your lips. Choose a shocking red that suits your colouring. Outline your lips with a same-shade lip pencil, bringing it fairly straight across your top lip to minimise the Cupid's bow. Then fill in with a lip brush.

When it comes to hair, severity is your watchword. Minimalist hair is sculptural. You never entertain frizz, flicks or ringlets. Start by straightening it with blowdryer or straightening irons, always remembering to apply a good thermal protection lotion first. Then draw a parting very deep on one side, sweep your hair across your forehead and add lots of shining serum. If you are more adventurous, try creating a sculptural bun using a bun ring (here we have made an over-sized ring cut from upholstery foam, but a normal bun ring is available from chemists). If your hair is shorter, scrape it back and pin on a fake bun.

How to do the Minimalist look

How to choose bright lipstick

Cool and bright

Your hair may be white blonde, ash blonde, cool mid brown, dark brown or black, but is definitely not red or auburn and has no hint of ginger or yellow. If your hair has gone grey, it has gone a true silver or salt-and-pepper.

Your skin is alabaster white, olive or black with no hint of red or freckles.

Your eyes are dark or have a dark rim around the iris.

Lip colours: Fuchsia, Wine, Pillar Box.

Warm

Your hair has a reddish cast. It could be anything from chestnut to auburn or ginger to strawberry blonde. If it has turned grey, it's a kind of yellowish grey that you can't wait to have coloured.

Your skin tone is sallow or freckly, generally not dark.

Your eyes may be pale blue, brown, hazel or dull green.

Lip colours: Tomato, Brick.

Mid tones

Your hair is in the mid tones – it may be dark blonde, mouse brown, mid brown or mid auburn. If your hair has gone grey, it's a soft, dull grey.

Your skin has blue undertones, it may be quite pale and washed out or you may have a peaches and cream complexion.

Your eyes are predominantly green, aqua or blue.

Lip colours: Fuchsia, Pillar Box.

A sculptural bun

Tie pony tail at the nape of the neck on the side, backcomb the ponytail.

Pull hair through and around to cover the whole bun ring.

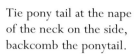

Pin into place underneath.

Tip: 'Play around with where you want your bun to be – the more off-centre, the more dramatic.'

HIGH
MAINTENANCE

YOU'RE EXPENSIVE AND SLICK

So you want to be High Maintenance today?

High maintenance – '*Emotionally (or otherwise) demanding*'.
CASSELL'S DICTIONARY OF SLANG

Today you feel like being profoundly selfish. And why not? You yearn for your manic world to turn inside and not out again so that you can focus on the one person who deserves pampering…yourself. It would be gorgeous to have a piece of Victoria Beckham's life where decisions concern which credit card to burn a sartorial hole in, or which Hollywood star to be best friends with on Friday. It would be fab not to have a care in the world. Imagine, if you suspected your partner of being unfaithful, you could just leg it with your tennis coach. The scandal might even get you into the gossip pages. There is great comfort to be taken from living life as a cliché. You know what is around the corner and by this token you can manipulate your world.

Oh, but…you don't have time to be selfish. More to the point, you don't have the bleeding cash. It takes hours and a fortune to gleam and exude affluence from every hand-stitched pocket. All those High Maintenance women that we love reading about, like Paris Hilton, Ivana Trump, Eva Longoria, et al, are in a position to demand constant attention. It's in their blood to stamp a high heel when they want something. Your mates are far too sincere to be taken in by a bronzed beacon of self indulgence who collects friends like clothes and dumps them when they have been seen out and about too often.

Oh, but…wouldn't it be wicked to live life through your hair extensions and discuss your Malibu tan with your colonic irrigationist. It would be so much fun to be deliberately tacky and wear one's recently acquired, or in this case fictitious, wealth on one's designer sleeve.

First of all, you get a weekend, don't you? Try High Maintenance for size on a Saturday. Book in for a manicure, pedicure, eyelash perm, Brazilian, spray tan, leg wax, eyebrow tint, teeth bleaching, hair highlighting, facial, botox, nail extensions or any of the above…High Maintenance is all about the outside.

It's all about the spit and polish of a bouncy blowdry and how much gloss you can apply to your plumped lips. You have spent a princely sum for a dress. That dress must be given the respect it deserves — a streamlined figure with no lumps and bumps (thank godmother for Magic Knickers). You can call everyone 'babe' and order coffee while screaming down your mobile? That's not so hard.

Because the High Maintenance girl is, well, rather fake, you can have such fun with her. It can be a real giggle to do it with other girlfriends. Look at the WAGS. They travel in packs and they seem to have a ball.

Life can be one endless social event.

High Maintenance wardrobe essentials

Clothes

- DESIGNER JEANS
- FITTED T-SHIRTS
- TIGHT MINI SKIRT
- WHITE SUITS
- DESIGNER LOGO T-SHIRTS
- FIGURE-HUGGING DRESS
- SHORT, BRIGHT COAT
- BOOT-CUT TROUSERS

Colour, pattern and texture

- TROPICAL PRINTS
- ANIMAL PRINTS
- BRIGHT ORANGE, TURQUOISE AND GREEN
- GOLD TRIM
- DESIGNER LOGOS
- CHIFFON
- CRYSTAL DECORATIONS
- CUT-OUT DETAILS

Take design inspiration from

- VERSACE
- ROBERTO CAVALLI
- HERVE LEGER
- DOLCE & GABBANA
- GUCCI

Daytime High Maintenance

A High Maintenance female is toned and groomed like a thoroughbred racehorse. Your aim is to show the world that you are well kept, that you have an extremely wealthy and powerful man in your life – or soon will have. If you are single, this may just be the way to land that elusive billionaire.

Fitted

Everything is always fitted, fitted, fitted. Even your t-shirts have been to the seamstress for a tummy tuck. The full-time High Maintenance girl practically lives with her trainer. If you are not sporting a washboard stomach, make sure that you have some great Magic Knickers to hold in any wobbles.

Jeans

A boot-leg cut shows your backside to best effect. Never wear your jeans with flat shoes – ankle boots or killer heels make your legs look endless. High Maintenance jeans are not ripped, torn or faded, rather they are dark denim, dry cleaned and perfectly pressed.

Jackets

High Maintenance jackets are very, very fitted, always nipped in to show off your waist. Wear a jacket with your jeans and make sure that it is short enough to show off your backside (and the logo on it). Team either with an open-necked blouse or a plain, fitted white t-shirt.

Day dresses

You can often be seen at lunch attired in a dress that others might choose for a cocktail party or wedding. It is sleeveless, to show off your shoulders, in a plain block colour and a rich fabric, like satin, heavy silk or stretch wool.

Separates

Your alternative to jeans and jacket is a fitted pencil skirt and a fitted, belted cardigan – always with a plunging V. Unlike the Ice Queen, you would always flash your lace bra.

'Use clever
underwear to
create a trim,
toned silhouette.'

'Work that
pearly smile
and front
page pout.'

Night-time High Maintenance

At night, you get out the full works: the heels, the jewels and, most of all, the designer labels. High Maintenance evening wear takes courage – there's a lot of flesh on show. It's all very well to wear bum-lifting, tummy-sucking foundation garments, but you must also practise standing erect, flashing your white teeth and flipping your tresses. If in doubt, hire your own paparazzo to follow you around for the evening, then check out the pictures.

Bra

You are not embarrassed about supplementing your assets, but it might be a trifle impractical to have a boob job just to get this look. A gel-filled plunge bra creates the perfect High Maintenance silhouette.

Evening gown

Your gown can be anything from full length to a micro mini, but it is always fitted to your body, showing off your arms, cleavage and any other assets you care to flaunt.

Coats

As High Maintenance, you dress for maximum impact every time you step out the door. You don't wear a coat to cover up, preferring instead to use it as a way of making an entrance. Even your raincoat is never a plain mac. A coat should be even more glitzy than your outfit underneath.

Legs

You would rather eat jellied eels than wear tights. Your legs are always on show. To that end, they are waxed, tanned (either real or fake) and moisturised until they glow.

Strappy sandals

Even in midwinter, brave the elements in open-toed shoes or strappy sandals. How else are you going to show off your perfect pedicure and tanned feet?

High Maintenance finishing touches

More than anything else, it's the finishing touches that give High Maintenance that aspirational, high-end feel. You're always decked out in the full array of designer sunglasses, handbag, belt, shoes and watch. Labels are to the fore so there's no mistaking where it all came from.

Make sure that your sunglasses have a noticeable logo. When it's windy, you can push your sunglasses up on your head to keep your hair from blowing onto your lip gloss.

Like everything High Maintenance, your watch says, 'Hey, look at how expensive I am.'

A High Maintenance handbag must be recognisably designer. Not some Cutting Edge new fashion, but one of the biggies: Fendi, Gucci, Dior, Louis Vuitton or, best of all, Hermès.

Whether it's their red soles, bridle motif or intertwined Cs, the most important thing about High Maintenance shoes is that they are definably designer.

As a High Maintenance gal, you love to wear jewellery so much that you never take it off – not for sentimental reasons but more to make sure that everyone knows how much your lover is worth, even when you're on the beach or in the gym.

'A giant rock is
the ultimate
High Maintenance
bauble.'

The classic High Maintenance earring is the giant hoop. They look great in amongst the gorgeous sweep of your hair. Equally, a pair of large, flashy diamond studs will attract attention.

High Maintenance is defined by high-shine lip gloss.

Summer or winter, it's vital to look like you have just been on a yacht or a ski slope. Keep your body glowing with a good quality fake tan and use a bronzing powder to add a sun-touched look to your face.

'Black Orchid', a scent by Tom Ford.

High Maintenance beauty

High Maintenance beauty is glitzy, glossy and glamorous. There's no pussyfooting around with make-up that pretends to be natural. Day or night, you are ready to be photographed on board a yacht or stepping out of a stretch limousine.

You are groomed, plucked, sprayed, shined and polished until it almost hurts. Your complexion is permanently South-of-France bronze and you skilfully apply contouring and highlighter so that your face catches its key light from any angle.

Use neutral tones to define your eyes, pale on the lid and brow bone, darker in the socket and under your eye. You are not averse to fakery, so add a few false eyelashes on top of your already curled and mascara-ed eyelashes.

Make sure that your lip gloss is so high beam that it could double as an aircraft navigation beacon.

Cultivate the impression that you hold a platinum loyalty card at the hairdresser with perfectly blowdried, bouncy hair. Use mousse for added body, and Velcro rollers or a big, round brush for maximum root lift. Finish with serum to give your hair shine and swing.

How to do the
High Maintenance look

Perfect
contouring

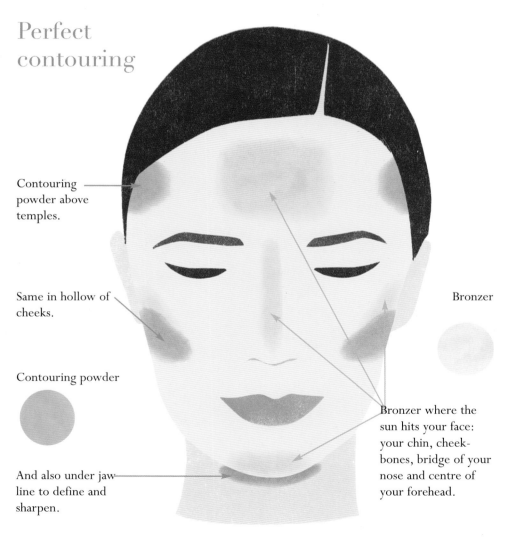

Contouring powder above temples.

Same in hollow of cheeks.

Contouring powder

And also under jaw line to define and sharpen.

Bronzer

Bronzer where the sun hits your face: your chin, cheekbones, bridge of your nose and centre of your forehead.

Big hair

Blowdry your hair straight. Once it is dry, divide it into sections. Hairspray each section and wrap it around a medium-sized Velcro roller.

Blast the whole lot with a hair dryer to set it, then leave to cool for 20-30 minutes.

Remove the rollers and brush your hair out gently.

BOHO
You're an arty fairy

So you want to be Boho today?

Boho — *Abbreviation of Bohemian, 'a socially unconventional person, especially an artist or writer'.*

OXFORD ENGLISH DICTIONARY

You have seen them in the magazines, those carefree girls with the wind in their hair and daisies between their toes. They don't stick to decaf coffee. They don't worry about matching their shoes to their handbag or paying the mortgage. They just go where the music takes them. You feel it now – a pent-up creativity that has been suppressed by the weight of relentless work and domestic obligations. A wanton mutineer is bubbling up inside and you decide to give convention the finger for a day.

But…you just can't let go. Your blowdry won't allow it. 'I'm too sensible,' you think. 'Too responsible,' you mutter. 'Too old,' you cry out loud. Don't be so uptight. Your level-headed side deserves a break. Prudence and sanity need to be put on the back burner so that you can find your inner child.

We wouldn't mind betting that you are ever-so-slightly bored with the boardroom and your school run duties. We put in so much effort protecting ourselves from negative forces and assuming an unruffled pose that sometimes our guard needs a good slap with a carpet beater.

Do you think Edie Sedgwick gave a hoot about what others thought? It's a huge relief to be shambolic occasionally, and if you dress with gay abandon you can get away with murder. Just look at Kate Moss. She's been doing it for years.

Joyful and free, you make your mind up to be little rebellious and devil-in-a-tutu-may-care. The time is ripe to mix the sensible you with Snow White and Sienna Miller. So jump up and don't make the bed, grab a slice of cold pizza for breakfast, lock the Blackberry in your kitchen drawer and get ready for your Boho moment.

A Boho chick is NOTHING without her dressing-up box of tricks. She mixes her clothes into a delicious concoction of alter-egos, eras and styles.

She will forget to clean her nails or brush her hair. Her socks and earrings will be odd and she will have reminders written all over her hand. This gives her the air of one harmlessly out of control. She is not in charge of her actions or feelings. If she does something bad, the world will forgive her because she is just so KOOKY.

A Boho's life is one big Glastonbury...music, mud and freedom.

Boho wardrobe essentials

Clothes

- IT'S MORE ABOUT HOW YOU PUT IT ALL TOGETHER THAN SPECIFIC ITEMS
- SMOCK DRESS
- LEGGINGS
- LONG HIPPY SKIRTS
- WAISTCOATS
- BIG CARDIGANS
- ANYTHING FROM A CHARITY SHOP

Colour, pattern and texture

- LAYERING
- MIXING PRINTS
- SMALL FLORAL PRINTS
- BRIGHT COLOURS
- PASTELS
- BRASS BUTTONS
- EMBROIDERY
- PRINTED CHIFFON
- CROCHET

Take design inspiration from

- PHILOSOPHY DI ALBERTA FERRETTI
- STELLA MCCARTNEY
- ANTIK BATIK
- BETSEY JOHNSON
- ANNA SUI

Daytime Boho

Take a pinch of sixties coffee-drinking, poetry-reading Bohemian, add a dash of seventies beaded, flowery Hippy and a soupçon of right now Cutting Edge Cool, throw it in the pot with a few vintage hats and Moroccan bangles and you have cooked yourself up a modern Boho.

Layering

The key to the Boho look is layering: a waistcoat, a gilet or a long, sleeveless coat will add a laid-back air when worn over a shirt or dress. Another way to achieve the layered look is to wear a shirt or long-sleeved top under your sleeveless dress.

Looseness

Boho is the polar opposite of High Maintenance. Your clothes are rarely fitted and you would not be seen dead in a suit. You found a fabulous floral tea dress in the market, but it's two sizes too big. So what? Pull it in to your waist with a wide, funky belt. If that divine Dior gown is too long, drag it through a few puddles. You aim to give the impression that your outfit came from the dressing-up box, not the designer floor of Harvey Nichols.

Jeans

They may be skinny, flared or cut off at the buttock, but Boho jeans are always personalised and lived in. You would no more iron your jeans than you would listen to Kylie records. Tailored trousers, of course, are for squares!

Tights

You love a bit of crazy leg wear. It adds a naughty schoolgirl element to your look. Try thick opaque tights, zig-zag patterned tights, tartan over-the-knee socks, stripey ankle socks – anything but sheer, natural tights.

'Layering
allows you to
wear all your
favourite
pieces at
once.'

'Boho brings
out your
playful side.'

Night-time Boho

As much as it looks just thrown together, it really takes a lot of studying in the mirror to look so gorgeously scruffy. Whereas High Maintenance will take sequins and fur and dress them up to the nines for a cocktail party, you will take the same and dress it down with wellies for a festival. The Boho look is young at heart, but it isn't about being young – it's about being really interesting and artistic. So, whatever your age, dive in without fear.

Vintage

As a Boho, you love vintage clothes but you also love to mix them up in a grungy way. Whereas the Avant-Garde Eccentric will wear a selection of exquisite pieces assembled like a museum display, your Boho sensibilities will mix an antique Victorian blouse with a pair of cut-off jeans and the latest Miu Miu heels.

Necklaces

Long necklaces make you seem leaner and taller. You can easily wear several together, mixing beads, chains and charms indiscriminately.

Evening wear

At night, a Boho never wants to look too glamorous or sophisticated. Dress down your glamorous gowns with opaque tights and wedges or platforms. Before going out at night look in the mirror and ask yourself, 'Is my hair messed up? Is my top missing a button? Is my jewellery looking eclectic and a bit random?' If the answer is yes, yes, yes, then you are fit to go.

Pattern and texture

Whatever you wear, you need to break it up by layering different textures and mixing multiple prints. While you love all prints and add in magpie bits of glitter and beading, what you cherish most is a sweet, tiny floral design. Your look is a walking confectionery, a delicious, kooky sweet shop for the eye.

Boho finishing touches

Boho's eclectic accessories definitely carry echoes of the sixties and seventies. While you are not a hippy, you are truly a free spirit, traipsing the world picking up a handbag in a market here, an ornate ring there, and mixing it up with some vintage sunglasses and the latest shoes from the catwalk.

In the Boho world, every day is sunny. So you need a pair of big, funky sunglasses. Make sure they are not recognisably designer – that would be most uncool.

As a Boho, you love to pick up bits of vintage glamour and mix them in with your outfit.

While a Boho might wear the latest platforms to a party, what you really love is to run free in sandals or flip-flops.

Your collection of bangles is more a history of where you've been and who you've seen than a fashion statement. Mix in a couple of friendship strings, some African beads and a backstage access band to complete the Boho effect.

You have spent the last week working at your job, as usual, but you want to give the impression that you've just come back from a Boho camping holiday by the sea. No problem. Spritz Bumble and bumble Surf Spray into your hair and rub some gorgeous bronzing oil onto your shoulders and legs.

The Boho look is fresh and easy. A light gloss is all that's needed on your lips. Apply little and often.

'Every day is
a holiday for
Boho girls.'

'Daisy', a scent
by Marc Jacobs.

Boho beauty

A Boho girl appears to skip through life with never a thought for grooming. You are too absorbed in reading Sartre, caring for abandoned animals and rushing off to poetry readings to be searching for your comb, your lipstick or your mobile phone.

Your favourite habitats are the beach and the tent so you cultivate a fresh, out-doorsy look. The Boho complexion has a healthy glow, and uses just enough foundation to conceal any blemishes. If you have great skin, a tinted moisturiser will do. Curl your lashes and then just add a lick of mascara.

At night your make-up is heavy and smoky on the eyes, but the Boho look is less harsh than the Rock Chick's. Stick with earthy tones and smudge with a cotton bud. Keep your lips free of colour, enhance them simply with lip balm during the day or gloss in the evening.

Bohos love to tiptoe through the tulips in flip-flops, sandals or bare feet, so use a daily exfoliator on your tootsies and for special occasions have a good pedicure and paint your toenails in baby pink.

Your hair looks effortless, as though the fairies danced in it all night long. But although it's messy, it's never actually a mess. Your dragged-through-a-hedge-backward coiffure is constructed with skill and artfulness. It's a style that will look great no matter how hard you dance.

How to do the Boho look

How to look youthful

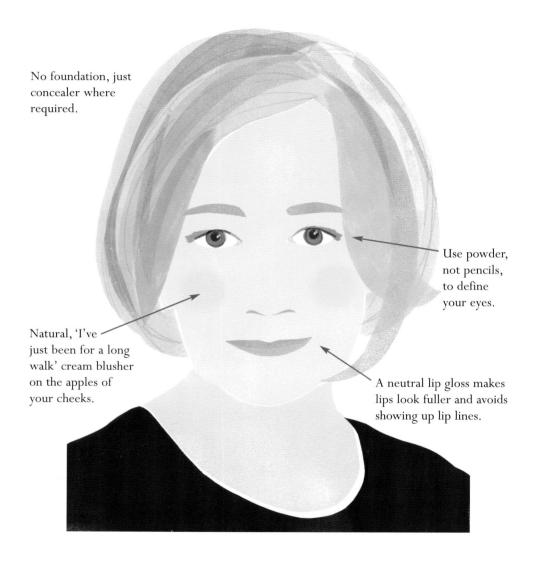

No foundation, just concealer where required.

Use powder, not pencils, to define your eyes.

Natural, 'I've just been for a long walk' cream blusher on the apples of your cheeks.

A neutral lip gloss makes lips look fuller and avoids showing up lip lines.

Boho twists

Divide your hair into about six little ponytail sections while it is still slightly damp.

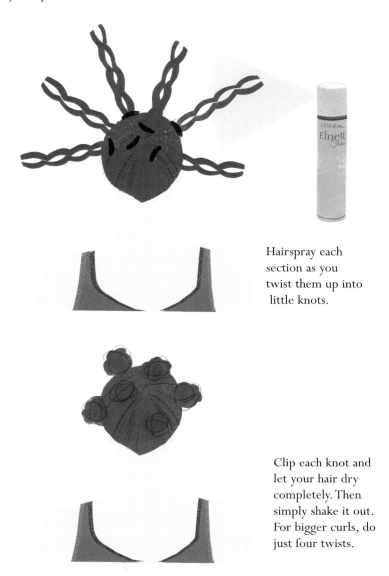

Hairspray each section as you twist them up into little knots.

Clip each knot and let your hair dry completely. Then simply shake it out. For bigger curls, do just four twists.

WHERE
TO LOOK

VINTAGE

Dandelion Vintage

Very charming vintage attire, particularly great for dresses. American pricing makes it so affordable you'll want to squeal. From Victorian era to 1980s. £
www.dandelionvintage.com

Hemlock Vintage Clothing

A very nicely presented vintage website with a descriptive paragraph for each item. There's a diverse collection, with clothes in good nick, and they have a discount section. They also sell vintage items for the home. £ – ££
www.hemlockvintage.com

Justsaywhen

Mostly designer vintage from the 20th century. A fantastic assortment from funky to fabulous. ££ – £££
www.justsaywhen.com

Posh Girl Vintage Clothing

An amazing selection of vintage clothing and accessories (and even lingerie if you're brave). Company is family owned and operated out of California, includes both designer and unknown labels, all in mint condition. ££
www.poshgirlvintage.com

Unique Vintage

Fun and hip site, offers a fab range of vintage designer-inspired women's clothing, at affordable prices. £ – ££
www.unique-vintage.com

Ver Unica

Based in San Francisco, this is a designer vintage store with a high-class list of clientele. Create an account and order online, or rush down there if you're in San Francisco. Not to be missed. £££
www.ver-unica.com

Vintage Trends

An easy to navigate site with a full range of men's and women's vintage, recycled, and military wear. Very affordable. £
www.vintagetrends.com

Vintage Vixen

Separated into occasion-appropriate sections, including wedding dresses. Very reasonable prices. £ – ££
www.vintagevixen.com

What Comes Around Goes Around

Unique vintage designer pieces and a collection of vintage-inspired numbers which adorn many stars; gives you access to New York's premiere vintage retailer. ££ – £££
www.nyvintage.com

When in London

Annie's Vintage Costume

Has a very antique feeling to it, stocked with white lace, slips and vintage silk. On the weekends there is an antique market through the entire passage. ££
12 Camden Passage N1.

Blackout II

Good quality authentic men's and women's vintage clothing, ranging from the 1920s through 1980s. ££
www.blackout2.com

Decades in Dover Street Market

You'll find this gem inside Dover Street's expansive, trendy designer warehouse. It is a mini boutique stocking very well selected vintage items. ££
www.doverstreetmarket.com

Grays Antique Market

Jewellery, corsets, Victorian lace nighties, bustles, ethnic prints, books, fabrics, and so much more. Beautiful items priced accordingly. ££
58 Davies Street, W1.

Heba

A very interesting concept boutique with some vintage items and some new designs – but all ultra cool. ££
164 Brick Lane E1.

Mensah

A small but particularly good selection of unique vintage designer pieces all in mint condition. They also stock some edgy contemporary designers who are just bursting onto the market. Well worth a look. ££
291 Portobello Road W11.
www.mensah.uk.com

One of a Kind

The coolest of A-list celebs apparently peruse these racks where the clothes, mostly designer, are inimitable and in pristine condition. The prices, of course, are demonstrative of this. £££
259 Portobello Road W11.

Orsini

Specialises in carefully selected one-off designer items from days gone by. Beautiful but rather expensive. ££
76 Earls Court Road W8.

Pop Boutique

Very cool 1970s and 1980s retro chic. £
www.pop-boutique.com

Rellik

This is the place for top-quality designer pieces. The clothes are exquisite vintage, if equally pricey. The website will give you the address but otherwise it is just a visual. ££ – £££
8 Golbourne Road W10.
www.relliklondon.co.uk

Rokit Vintage

This store can be a touch over-priced but they have a very funky, young and hip selection of coats, furs, boots, belts, dresses, etc. £ – £££
Shops at 101 Brick Lane E1, 255 Camden High Street NW1 and 42 Shelton Street WC2.
www.rokit.co.uk

Steinberg and Tolkien

Rare and one-off designer clothing. It's very pricey but worth it if you are looking for a really special item. £££
193 Kings Road SW3.

This Shop Rocks

A plethora of dresses along with some lovely antique dolls and bric-a-brac. Just adorable. ££
131 Brick Lane E1.

Virginia

Film noir-esque shop with lots of silk and lace and luxe. Be sure to call in advance as the store is not always open to the public. £££
98 Portland Road W11. 020 7727 9908.

When in USA

C. Madeleine's

This huge Miami vintage extravaganza is 10,000 square feet and sells clothing from the last 100 years. You are as likely to snag a fantastic little dress for under £20 as you are a designer jacket for nearly £2000. An institution to be sure and oft frequented by film stylists. £ – £££
www.cmadeleines.com

Frock NYC

Well selected designer pieces and an easy to use website with great descriptions of each item. You cannot order online but you can email or call after perusing images. £££
www.frocknyc.com

Resurrection

Vintage stores based in Los Angeles and New York City. Frequented by A-list celebs and designers alike. Designer vintage wear in pristine condition, well worth a look for inspired one-of-a-kinds but the website isn't the easiest to navigate. £££
www.resurrectionvintage.com

When in Paris

Didier Ludot

Haute couture vintage wear. The website is very high-tech and offers a beautiful photo-montage of the stock, but you must go and visit one of the shops (the main branch being on the rue de Rivoli in Paris) to purchase. £££
www.didierludot.com

MARKETS

When in Italy

Florence – San Lorenzo Market
Anything beautiful and leather you ever wanted. Bargaining is key. Every day.
Piazza Del Mercato Centrale by San Lorenzo Church and the Duomo

Rome – Porto Portese Market
Clothes both new and second-hand: amazing furs, leather, and jeans. The antiques and jewellery are also worth looking into. Sunday.
Piazza Ippolito Nievo, Trastevere 00153

When in Paris

Les Puces de Saint-Ouen
Allegedly the biggest flea market in the world with fairground energy; haggling will get you everywhere. On offer is everything from 1970s leather jackets to Louis XVI chests; also some lovely antique jewellery. Saturday–Monday. 18th arrondissement.

Malik Market
The clothing and jewellery haven within Saint-Ouen (above).

Marché aux Puces de Montreuil
Second-hand clothes and bric-a-brac, this is a massive and diverse flea market. Saturday-Monday. 20th arrondissement

Marché aux Puces de la Porte de Vanves
A feast for the imagination and a truly French experience, this market covers a wide range of inspirational vintage clothes, jewellery and antiques. Weekends. 14th arrondissement

When in London

Camden Lock
Arts and crafts, jewellery, second-hand clothing; more upmarket items are inside the Victorian market hall. Saturday and Sunday.
Near Camden Town station, NW1.

Brick Lane
Streets lined with stallholders selling anything and everything you could imagine; great for eccentric and cheap jewellery. Sunday.
Brick Lane, E1.

The Backyard Market
Artisans of all trades flock here to display their wares and you will find some of the most affordable and interesting jewellery and accessories here. Sunday.
Brick Lane, E1.

Spitalfields
An indoor market with a host of new and emerging designers. Here you will find clothes and jewellery, but also great nick-nacks and books and even music. Monday-Sunday.
Commercial Street, E1.

HIGH STREET

Petticoat Lane

Hundreds of stalls selling discounted clothing, Asian fabrics and leatherwear. Monday-Sunday. Middlesex Street, E1.

Portobello Road

The street is lined with stalls of jewellery, clothes, household items and antiques. Towards the top of the road there is a covered section of new designers and vintage clothing stalls. Portobello is world famous for a reason but prices are starting to represent this. Saturdays to get it all, but the market functions to some extent on Friday and Sunday as well. Portobello Road, W10 & 11

Abercrombie & Fitch

Young and fun clothes, best for those basic casual pieces and jeans. Order online or use the store locator. £–££
www.abercrombie.co.uk

Accessorize

This is a key stop-off point for everyone – accessories make a look unique and here you will find everything you ever wanted, at very friendly prices. £
www.accessorize.co.uk

Aldo

A great selection of the latest trends are on display here. While the prices are fairly reasonable, quality can be questionable. Website is user-friendly, shipping worldwide. £ – ££
www.aldoshoes.com

All Saints

Cool selection of clothes that are often quite edgy. The style is pretty-girly meets grungy rock-chick, and you can use the website to order online for deliveries all over the world. ££
www.allsaintsshop.co.uk

American Apparel

All the basics and then some. Well crafted, not from sweatshops, and some funky designs in big and bold colours and wild fabrics. The store windows are pure Cutting Edge Cool, but individually items can form the foundation of many different looks. £
www.americanapparel.net

Appletree Boutique

As the name suggests, this is a very sweet shop, with unique home accessories and a fun selection of frilly dresses and tops. £
127 and 164 Portobello Road W11

Banana Republic

Elegant fashions will suit those channeling Sophisticate sensibilities. While it isn't cheap, for some beautiful staple pieces it's worth the spend. ££
www.bananarepublic.eu

Bodas

Beautiful quality undergarment and nightwear that is very sophisticated and feminine. ££
www.bodas.co.uk

Boden

Sweet items, leaning more towards the Gamine, Ice Queen, and Sophisticate styles. The website features a unique "Outfit Ideas" section. £ - ££
www.boden.co.uk

Bravissimo

Affordable bras, swimwear and clothes that cater to big breasted women. They stock up to an H cup, and still manage to be very pretty. £
www.bravissimo.com

Coast

The perfect go-to place for a cocktail dress with a twist. Prices are reasonable and the variety of styles ensures that every body shape can be flattered. Particularly suitable for High Maintenance, Ice Queen and Sophisticate looks on a budget. £ – ££
www.coast-stores.com

Cos

Fashion essentials that would appeal to Minimalist, Gamine and Androgyne looks in particular. You can look at the collections on line, but you must use the store locator and purchase these high-fashion items in person. ££
www.cosstores.com

Diesel

The coolest of cool denim, with an extensive variety, though best suited for slim figures. They also have skirts, dresses, tops, bags, perfume and sunglasses. Not exactly cheap, but generally very good quality. ££
www.diesel.com

Dorothy Perkins

Very feminine clothes at friendly prices. Downside is that there is loads to sift through. £
www.dorothyperkins.co.uk

Evans

Plus size women's wear that is very affordable, though the styles can be quite uniform and not always inspiring. £
www.evans.co.uk

Faith

A fun and diverse selection of footwear for just about any occasion – including bridal. £
www.faith.co.uk

French Connection

Simple elegance and subtle flare, this shop is reliable for cocktail dresses, beautiful jackets, and floaty dresses. The clothes are well-tailored and made to last, and the website is designed to make your shopping as easy as possible. ££
www.frenchconnection.com

Gap

All your basic needs will be satisfied here. While their clothes may not always be overly exciting, you can look very clean and chic on a tight budget. £
www.gap.com

H&M

The "Dressing Room" function allows you to put your face on a model and try on clothes, but you can't purchase on the site. If you want modish and cheap clothes, this is the place to go. Quality is questionable but at this price it doesn't really matter. £
www.hm.com

Hobbs

The use of colour in their styles is commendable, however the clothing can lean towards staid. Their leatherwear, particularly boots, is the most useful and reliable. ££
www.hobbs.co.uk

Jaeger

The online catalogue has very helpful suggestions as to how to put outfits together, and the clothes are becoming more and more hip. Good tailoring and some attention to detailed decorations go a long way towards making this traditionally conservative store appealing. ££
www.jaeger.co.uk

Jigsaw

You can't shop on the website but it will direct you to your nearest shop, where you will find classy formal and work wear combined with funky casual clothes. Their use of colour is always excellent and the quality is top-notch. Also look out for stylish shoes, boots, lingerie and bags. ££
www.jigsaw-online.com

John Smedley

Good quality, basic knitwear. Merino wool twin-sets that will make an Ice Queen melt. ££
www.johnsmedley.com

Karen Millen

High Maintenance on a budget. The clothes here are detail oriented and eye-catching. Great for suits and evening wear as they have lots of snazzy going-out dresses. ££
www.karenmillen.com

Kurt Geiger

Splendid selection of shoes, from Chloé and Marc Jacobs to their own slightly less expensive line. All the latest trends are on display. ££
www.kurtgeiger.com

La Redoute

An online catalogue of the best of French high-street fashion. A veritable plethora of choice! £
www.laredoute.com

Lee

Jeans jeans jeans! They fit well and come in all shapes, not just the trend du jour. ££
www.lee.com

Levi's

The original American denim company, they still know what's up. Denim to satisfy all your needs. ££
www.levisstores.com

Littlewoods

Something for everyone – a range of high-street and midrange brands, and designs exclusive to the site – including our very own range. Use the genius-inspired "Shape Advisor" to find clothes that flatter your body shape. £ – ££
www.littlewoods-direct.com or call 0844 822 8000

LK Bennett

Classic styles and bright fabrics make this store a place for Sophisticates and Ice Queens on a bold day. Very feminine, if slightly conservative, and they also make good quality shoes. ££
www.lkbennett.com

Mango

This Spanish chain now has a line from Penelope Cruz and her sister. The items are high-fashion and very affordable, but are likely to last only as long as the trend does. A huge selection, and be sure to check out their shoes and accessories. £
www.mango.com

Marks & Spencer

A brilliant store for underwear, hosiery, and other basic necessities. The clothes can border on frumpy, but they are always trying to revamp their look – and with some success. Certainly worth a careful look. £
www.marksandspencer.com

Massimo Dutti

Well-tailored clothes tending towards classic casual. A nice use of luxurious fabrics in easy to wear styles, will up your elegance factor with ease. ££
www.massimodutti.co.uk

Mikey London

Fun and cheap fashion jewellery, sunglasses and handbags. The website is very well organised and very user-friendly and the bargains are superb. £
www.mikeyjewellery.co.uk

Miss Selfridge

Flirty and funky styles certain to satisfy youthful frivolity. A very accessible and helpful website. £
www.missselfridge.com

Miss Sixty

Revealing and trendy clothes explicitly designed to ooze sex appeal. Their fashions can be tricky to pull off without a fabulous figure, however. ££
www.misssixty.com

Monsoon

A very detailed and accessible site. The clothes are most obviously suitable for Gamine, Ice Queen and Sophisticate looks, though with creativity and the right accessories anything is possible. A perfect shop to hit-up in search of formal wear, and most of their styles go up to a size 24. £
www.monsoon.co.uk

My Tights

Hosiery heaven! Shop online by style, type or brand of tights. Also, they stock our very own Magic Knickers to ensure any outfit looks its best on you. £
www.mytights.com

New Look

Young, fresh, and inexpensive fashions; great for party wear. Be sure to keep an eye out for celebrity collections, as well. £
www.newlook.co.uk

Next

Practical and good quality, this shop is particularly good for tailoring and office wear as well as solid basics. £
www.next.co.uk

Nine West

Comfortable and relatively affordable shoes. Their designs very wearable. £ – ££
www.ninewest.com

Oasis

Finger-on-the-pulse styles, both casual and pretty. Great for bags, shirts, swimwear and accessories. £ – ££
www.oasis-stores.com

Office

Shoes in every style for every occasion, though certainly always with one eye on the latest trends. Very affordable, with great sales, but sometimes quality is lacking. £
www.office.co.uk

Pepe

Very cool, laid back fashion, with unexpected touches of luscious extravagance or edgy grunge. Shirts, dresses and denim are their strong points. £ – ££
www.pepejeans.com

Primark

The prices are so cheap you'll think they've made a mistake. With patience and ingenuity you can leave with an entire outfit for £20 that looks like it cost a whole lot more. The website is a store locator, not for online shopping. £
www.primark.co.uk

Principles

A great range of styles with sizes ranging from petite up to size 18. Helpful website. Particularly good for dresses. £
www.principles.co.uk

Reiss

Cool and classy collections that include lovely party dresses, well-cut trousers, and smart coats. Excellent combinations of neutral pallets with a splash of interesting, eye-catching colour. ££
www.reiss.co.uk

River Island

The site has a "Get the Latest Look" section for some inspirations on the latest trends. A wide range of styles covered here. £
www.riverisland.com

Russell & Bromley

Big shoe store that has fantastic quality and reliable boots every year. But for a high-street store the prices are quite high. ££
www.russellandbromley.co.uk

7 For All Mankind

Fantastic jeans to flatter any shape, with denim that only gets better the more it is worn. ££
www.7forallmankind.com

Schuh

A fab shoe store with a vast array of styles and brands to suit anyone from the young and hip, to more mature and conservative. £
www.schuhstore.co.uk

Shoe Studio

A surplus of high-street shoes all in one location. £
www.shoestudio.com

Ted Baker

Really great women's wear collection that fits well, is not boring, nor too reliant on trends. ££
www.tedbaker.com

TK Maxx

With persistence one can find hidden gems amidst the masses of designer rejects that fill the many racks. Options and sizes vary by the designer and what gets handed off, but there is always a plethora of stuff. £ – ££
www.tkmaxx.com

Toast

Lovely items on an easy to navigate site. A place to check out particularly for Minimalist, Boho, and Gamine days. ££
www.toast.co.uk

Topshop

The fashionistas' heaven. Topshop's website has a store locator as well as an online catalogue. It's easy to navigate and there's something for everyone, including celebrity collections and great designer knock-offs. Deliveries all over the UK, to North America, and to Australia/New Zealand. £
www.topshop.co.uk

DESIGNER & BOUTIQUES

Urban Outfitters

The Boho chick's haven, though certainly Cutting Edge Cool, Gamine, Rock Chick and even Eccentric styles could benefit here too. The online store has a decent selection but the shops have much more to offer. £ – ££
www.urbanoutfitters.co.uk

Wallis

Attractive and appealing styles for safer dressing. Good use of colour and classic shapes to flatter all different figures. £
www.wallis-fashion.com

Warehouse

Easy to wear and eye-catching fashions and accessories. Mostly quite relaxed clothes, but some good party dresses and holiday wear. £
www.warehouse.co.uk

Whistles

Ultra-feminine and pretty clothes. Particularly nice tailoring and lots of frills and ribbons – the Ice Queen will have her choice of tea dresses. ££
www.whistles.co.uk

Zara

The mecca that revolutionized high-street fashion. Zara is the go-to spot for of-the-second styles, as well as business wear and more casual day-to-day items. A reliable shop for basics as well as emergency occasion dressing – you are certain to find something. £ – ££
www.zara.com

Accessories Online

A plethora of amazing accessories from designers including Butler & Wilson, Les Nereides, and many more. ££
www.accessoriesonline.co.uk

Agent Provocateur

Kinky sexy undergarments, full stop. Expensive, but if you can afford it, so worth it. ££
www.agentprovocateur.com

Agnès b

Très chic French styling, particularly good for unique separates. Great for achieving that "Oh I just threw this on without thinking but look to die for" look. ££
www.agnesb.com

Aimé

French fashion and design for all your lifestyle needs – the best France has to offer. Here you will find bags, shoes, perfume, candles, boots, and more. ££
www.aimelondon.com

Angel Jackson

Fantastic individual bags, which range from eye-catching conversation pieces to day-to-day staples. ££
www.angeljackson.com

Anya Hindmarch

Creative and classy bags of all shapes and sizes. £££
www.anyahindmarch.com

APC

Straight from France, perfect for Gamine and Boho looks, clean and fresh website with sweet and fun clothes. ££ – £££
www.apc.fr

Arrogant Cat

A London boutique on Kensington Church Street but online ordering is simple here. Clothes are pictured from every angle to get the full effect. It's fun and fancy, party dress central, and a mecca for the High Maintenance crew – but good luck getting any sizes above a UK 12. ££
www.arrogantcat.com

Aquascutum

Top of the line trench coats and raincoats. Beautiful styles, impeccable tailoring. £££
www.aquascutum.co.uk

Baby Ceylon

Hand-crafted and dyed floaty feminine wear that will make you feel sexy, comfortable and quite cool. The great thing about the website is the write-ups on each item wherein they discuss which body-shape it might suit best. ££
www.babyceylon.com

Balenciaga

Very structural and quite severe, these designs are beautiful and fierce. £££
www.balenciaga.com

Belinda Robertson

Gorgeous cashmere jumpers on demand, choose your own bespoke colour, delivered right to your doorstep. Not cheap but made in Scotland, not China. ££ – £££
www.belindarobertson.com

Betsey Johnson

A little kooky and over the top, but these designs are just so much fun. Party dresses and accessories that will get you noticed and make you smile. £££
www.betseyjohnson.com

Bottega Veneta

Gorgeous shoes, bags and clothes that evoke old-fashioned holidays on the French Riviera. £££
www.bottegaveneta.com

Brora

Cashmere galore! Every colour imaginable, every style of sweater, scarf, and many other luxurious items. ££
www.brora.co.uk

Browns

Designer surfeit! If you can indulge, they cover the whole range of high-end designers. £££
www.brownsfashion.com

Bunny Hug

Choose from an abundance of youthful and trendy designers and labels, from Cheap Monday jeans to Splendid. ££
www.bunnyhug.co.uk

Butler & Wilson

This jewellery store is like a treasure trove, full of over the top glitz and glory. ££
www.butlerandwilson.co.uk

C & C California

They use only the softest fabrics to create these fantastic basics. The vests and long-sleeved shirts are particularly fab for their length. ££
www.candccalifornia.com

Chica

Like a waltz through your hip party friend's bedroom – jewellery, dresses and shoes, oh my! ££
www.chicaonlineboutique.com

Chloé

These designs are very hip and cool and have mastered the art of texture and structure. £££
www.chloe.com

Christian Louboutin

With the signature red soles and impeccable designs, these shoes are so worth the investment for sexy, classy style. £££
www.christianlouboutin.fr

Cinnamon Fashion

A great site that accommodates sizes 16–34, though choose with care as some of the styles can be dodgy and less than flattering. ££
www.cinnamonfashion.co.uk

Coco Ribbon

Such a girly store, and so much fun! The upstairs has nick-nacks and home stuff to add a little pretty-pretty to your bedroom. Follow the winding stairs down and you enter the clothing room – trouble for those lacking in self-restraint. A good selection from a variety of mid-range designers, and lots of beautiful party dresses. ££
www.cocoribbon.com

Darimeya Shop

Once just a stall on Portobello Road, they have now opened their own boutique. These adorable items have adorned the likes of Kate Moss and Sienna Miller, and this is the mecca for cute Gamine dresses (though Boho ladies will no doubt find it equally irresistible). ££
www.darimeya.co.uk

Diane von Furstenberg

The queen of the wrap dress, well worth a visit when in the mood to splash out on a dress that is guaranteed to be made of beautiful and interesting fabric, and figure-flattering shapes. Now also has a maternity range. ££
www.dvflondon.com

Diva

Masters of the corset dress, Divas and Bombshells will be in heaven. Very well crafted, very sexy, made-to-measure garments that will show off your figure and make you feel like a million quid, particularly if you have curves. ££
www.divacorsets.com

Dover Street Market

So hip it hurts, this shop is full of sass and funk displaying many items from up-and-coming designers. A Cutting Edge Cool paradise. £££
www.doverstreetmarket.com

Dragana Perisic

A boutique with lovely and unique gloves and jewels, and a small but interesting selection of clothes. ££
www.draganaperisic.com

Egg

Top-quality classic fabrics are used to create crisp, comfortable, sharp items that are very modern, easy to wear and nice to look at. This is the go-to place for Minimalist and Cutting Edge Cool looks. £££
www.eggclothing.com

Fairy Goth Mother

Don't be scared by the name, this is the place to head if you are feeling the need for some seriously sexy (under)clothes. They make corsets to order, but have a massive selection on display, and ruffles, bows, silk and satin galore. Bombshells and Divas eat your heart out! ££
www.fairygothmother.com

Fashion Net

Self-proclaimed "guide to all things chic" one might also add "cool" to that statement. In terms of shopping you can choose by designer or label. ££
www.fashion.net

Figleaves

A massive selection of underwear and swimwear from a range of brands, including some designer labels. Some styles are available in very large sizes (48-56 FF for example). They also stock maternity bras, and they deliver with speed. £
www.figleaves.com

Georgina Goodman

Cutting Edge shoes which you could display in your living room as a sculptures. They are just so cool! £££
www.georginagoodman.com

Gina

Diamenté and stiletto heals are a consistent feature on these designs. The shoes are slightly Diva meets High Maintenance but certainly are very sexy. £££
www.gina.com

Hoss Intropia

An inspired collection of clothing, handbags, and accessories, this new designer label is one to watch. Attention to detail and creative designs look you have spent an absolute fortune, when in fact the prices are quite reasonable. ££
www.hossintropia.com

Hoxton Boutique

A very fashion forward store. Their own line, Hobo, is fun and flirty, where Cutting Edge Cool and Boho collide. Stop by the gallery-store to check out all of the hip designers they stock; clothing, shoes and accessories galore. ££
www.hoxtonboutique.co.uk

Iris

Carrying shoes by Chloé, Marc Jacobs and others, what is particularly unique about this boutique is that they choose to stock entire lines from a designer. £££
www.iris-shoes.it

Isaac Mizrahi

Elegant, chic, structured yet luxurious, this designer is one to watch for Minimalist, Sophisticate and possibly Gamine and Androgyne looks. £££
www.isaacmizrahiny.com

Jimmy Choo

The ultimate in High Maintenance heels as well as classic court shoes in all heights. £££
www.jimmychoo.com

Joseph

Gamines and Sophisticates this is your one-stop shop. Clothes have very clean lines and well made staples for your wardrobe. You can't purchase online, however they do have stores all over the world. ££
www.joseph.co.uk

Kabiri

They stock both fashion and precious jewellery from all sorts of designers. The price range is vast so you can be sure to find something interesting in your budget. £ – £££
www.kabiri.co.uk

Kerry Taylor Auctions

If you're a serious fashion collector you need to bookmark this site.
www.kerrytaylorauctions.com

Koci Koci and Margo London

Sweet, girly and romantic styles by two sisters. The website is aesthetically pleasing but technically irritating, though a visit to the store is certainly worth your time. Margo London is an offshoot line which is more expensive and includes lovely lingerie. ££
www.kocikoci.com
www.margolondon.com

Koh Samui

Up-and-coming designers are here given a chance to shine. They also provide all the old favourites from Balenciaga to Marc Jacobs. £££
www.kohsamui.co.uk

LA Star Style

High Maintenance celeb-obsessed trend-followers start salivating now. You will find all the latest and greatest trends here, with photos of celebrities wearing the items they stock. £££
www.lastarstyle.com

Laundry Industry

Occasionally edgy and avant-garde, though equally pretty and chic, this line of clothes is interesting and innovative. You must be a registered member to shop online, but there are a number of boutiques around the world as well. ££
www.laundryindustry.com

Lulu Guinness

The queen of quirky couture bags, purses, clutches and vanity cases. Beautiful designs always likely to be attention grabbing. £££
www.luluguinness.com

Manolo Blahnik

Legendary footwear genius, these shoes make a statement and are as much for traipsing around as they are future museum pieces. £££
www.manoloblahnik.com

Marc Jacobs

Designs are very structural, embodying highly sophisticated, effortless elegance. £££
www.marcjacobs.com

Marni

Very cool and fun clothes that always possess a unique twist. £££
www.marni.com

Matches

A great selection of old-favourite and A-list designers to choose from that will save you the time of going to each store individually, but rapidly burn a hole in your wallet. £££
www.matchesfashion.com

Miame

This boutique has some very fun items that do occasionally border on bizarre. Be sure to check out the jewellery. ££
172 Brick Lane, London E1

MiMi

Chic boutique that specialises in evening wear. They stock clothing, shoes, bags, and jewellery from all sorts of designers and high-end labels. £££
www.mimilondon.co.uk

Miu Miu

Known for its exciting and directional yet highly wearable designs, this sweet, sexy and funky line from Miuccia Prada has particularly noteworthy shoes. £££
www.miumiu.com

My Wardrobe.com

Shop by designer, of which there are many, or by desired item. Very user-friendly. ££ – £££
www.my-wardrobe.com

Nancy Pop

Sophisticate meets Cutting Edge Cool in this relatively new designer boutique. They stock their own collection but also have exclusive rights to some new designers. All in all, amazing clothes that cover a range of prices and purposes. ££ – £££
www.nancypop.com

Net-a-Porter

The latest in designer shoes, bags, accessories, and clothing, with great sale options. Better for people with cash to burn, and likely to become an addiction on High Maintenance days. £££
www.net-a-porter.com

Not on the High Street

Detailed product information and a massive range of items, from home stuff to clothing. Certainly you will be able to find some fun basics and inspirational stuff on this easy to use website. ££
www.notonthehighstreet.com

Orla Kiely

Brightly coloured, fun fabrics define this designer. With a nice range of outerwear, dresses, and tops, you can also find cool retro-looking accessories, bags, luggage, wallpaper, stationery, and more. ££
www.orlakiely.com

Paul & Joe

With a lot of floaty and floral looks, there is also an air of effortless elegance to this line's designs. ££
www.paulandjoe.com

Pollyanna

An independent designer retailer which has an impeccable selection. It's the first UK stockist of Comme des Garçons, and a particularly good resource for Androgyne and Minimalist looks. £££
www.pollyanna.com

Poste Mistress

A fantastic shoe store that has a well-rounded and eclectic stock ranging from Vivienne Westwood to Birkenstock. ££
www.pmistress.co.uk

Prada

This legendary fashion house is considered one of the most influential in the industry. Their leatherwear and fashion-forward designs are pretty, quirky, eccentric and beautifully crafted. Shoes are actually comfortable as well as exquisite to look at! £££
www.prada.com

Public Beware Co.

Indeed, beware of letting yourself loose in this amazingly Cutting Edge Cool paradise: your wallet could take a lashing. ££
7 Dray Walk E1

Question Air

A hotspot for High Maintenance designer jeans of all shapes, sizes, and denim. This shop also offers a great range of fun items to add flare to any outfit. ££
www.question-air.com

Rigby & Peller

The ultimate lingerie store that provides the best bra fitting in town. They will cater for any breast size and offer a made-to-measure bra service. £££
www.rigbyandpeller.com

Roger Vivier

Very French chic shoes and bags. £££
www.rogervivier.com

Satine

Great LA boutique that is also online; trendy labels with very fun clothes any hipster would drool over, but shipping is pricey. The best part is the subheadings, including "Looks We Love" and "Items We Idolize." ££ – £££
www.satineboutique.com

Sexy Panties and Naughty Knickers

The name is an accurate, description of what is on offer here. Very detailed and lovely underwear. ££
www.sexypantiesandnaughtyknickers.com

Source

Fab boutique with great clothes and inspirational homes stuff. ££
www.sourcelifestyle.com

Souvenir

A fantastically jam-packed little store with Japanese-inspired designs alongside Vivienne Westwood and Viktor & Rolf. £££
www.souvenirboutique.co.uk

Spirito

Classic clothing for sizes 14-30.
www.spirito.co.uk

Start

With their finger on the pulse of all the latest trends, this store is always interesting. Parading new and hip designers alongside tried and trusted old friends, it should not be missed. £££
www.start-london.com

Sub Couture

Designer items from last season at significantly reduced prices. While each piece is generally a one-off in this shop, you are always likely to find something that works for any style or body shape. ££
204 Kensington Park Road W11

Sunglasses UK

A massive selection of all the most prominent designer's sunglasses, you really have your choice here. £ – ££
www.sunglassesuk.com

Tatty Devine

Very fun and creative jewellery that can border on the silly and childlike. Certainly a pit-stop on the hunt for a casual conversation piece. £ – ££
www.tattydevine.com

Temperley

This London-based designer is known for making very pretty, sophisticated garments with a twist. They have also recently expanded with a wonderful leather range. £££
www.temperleylondon.com

The Lazy Ones

These designs are sold at Topshop but get them here for less, with more selection. Very cute, original and lovely prints, textures, and colours and some bits and bobs to complete the vibe. £ – ££
www.thelazyones.com

The Shop at Bluebird

This concept boutique sells everything from womenswear and menswear to books and home deco stuff. A constantly evolving range of items makes this an exciting place to peruse. The website will give you a taste and direct you there, but you cannot purchase online. £££
www.theshopatbluebird.com

The West Village

A gorgeous selection of dresses, denim, outerwear and select vintage pieces make this shop a lovely Boho hotspot. In true bohemian form, however, the website is useless. ££
www.thewestvillage.co.uk

Twenty8Twelve

Sienna and Savannah Miller's brainchild produces clothes that are what you would expect from such fashion mavens. Edgy, pretty frocks mixed with a bit of bohemian grunge, occasionally over the top, mostly quite expensive. £££
www.twenty8twelve.com

Viva La Diva

From designer to high-street, this shoe mecca houses casual, trendy and dressy styles, all under one roof. £
www.vivaladiva.com

Wolford Boutique

Arguably the best tights out there, this line also offers undergarments of all sorts and they are reliable for being top quality. £££
www.wolfordboutiquelondon.com

Yoox

Every designer you've ever heard of, in a virtual boutique fashion extravaganza, though the excess of items can feel overwhelming if you don't have something specific in mind. ££ – £££
www.yoox.com

@ Work

Very cool jewellery store that has a variety of up-and-coming designers' work on display. They also offer classes, if you're in the mood to get creative. ££
www.atworkgallery.co.uk

127 Brick Lane

A very original, very cool (Cutting Edge for certain) boutique that's so hip it hurts. With a stock of one-off designer pieces, Rock Chicks and Minimalists could easily have a go here as well. The shop is full of conversation pieces. ££
127 Brick Lane E1

DEPARTMENT STORES

Debenhams
A more conservative and middle of the road department store, there are still some great finds to be had. The lingerie section is fantastic, and the website offers tips on how to dress for your body shape, as well as specialist clothing lines for petites, plus sizes, and maternity wear. ££.
www.debenhams.com

Harvey Nichols
This designer fashion emporium stocks all of the coolest top designers and some less expensive ones as well. The perfume and beauty hall is extensive and addictive. £££.
www.harveynichols.com

Harrods
The most famous of all department stores, Harrods maintains a conservative air but also has the best shoe department in Europe, stocking large and small sizes as well as an extensive choice of designers. It is often thronged with tourists. £££.
www.harrods.com

House of Fraser
Mostly mainstream labels with a few cool items to stumble upon. ££.
www.houseoffraser.co.uk

John Lewis
Though not often overly exciting, this store is great for affordable basics. The website has different ways of searching for clothes, including trends and events, which is unique. ££.
www.johnlewis.com

Liberty
Liberty is the gemstone of department stores, stocking only the latest, hippest and most beautiful of everything. They also have the largest collection of Vivienne Westwood in the city, among many, many other fashion labels. A joy to peruse. £££.
www.liberty.co.uk

Selfridges
The most enormous and dense selection of fashion, from high-street to high-end. It can be confusing and it's easy to get lost or simply pass out from fashion overload, but this store is generally considered to have its finger on the pulse of trends. Great for label-lovers, and the undergarment selection is massive. £ – £££.
www.selfridges.com

TREATS

Caravan

Kitsch done right – so sweet and original with a touch of the flamboyant. It's like a flea market in a store, where all the junk has already been weeded out. A handful of special clothing items, but mostly home décor and nick-nacks.
www.caravanstyle.com

Cupcakes and Bakes

Specialised cupcake service, delivers all over mainland UK.
www.cupcakesandbakes.com

Hotel Chocolat

Smart chocolate for aficionados.
www.hotelchocolat.co.uk

Hummingbird Bakery

The sweetest shop, selling a range of delicious and adorable cupcake treats. Order in advance for deliveries around London.
www.hummingbirdbakery.com

Maison Bertaux

This innovative café also has a lovely store inside it that sells some key designer clothes items, candles, jewellery, and more.
www.shopatmaisonb.com

Only Roses

They only stock roses, in all colours. So pretty, so unique, so expensive. Only the best quality. Delivery services available.
257 Old Brompton Road SW5.
020 7373 9595.

Rococo ChocolateS

The original decadent, fancy chocolate shop.
www.rococochocolates.com

BEAUTY

Angela Flanders Perfumer
Stocked full of delights like scented candles, lotions and bespoke perfumes.
www.angelaflanders-perfumer.com

Aveda
Plant-based products; the hair care is among the best out there.
www.aveda.co.uk

BeneFit
This much-loved beauty brand is famed for its cute and quirky packaging, and iconic make-up.
www.benefitcosmetics.co.uk

Bliss
You can't help but love this huge range of fun and funky body and skincare.
www.blisslondon.co.uk

Bumble and bumble
A great range of products and a store locator.
www.bumbleandbumble.com

By Terry
An amazing range of make-up and skincare by the genius who created Yves Saint Laurent's iconic Touche Eclat!
www.byterry.com

Eight Square
Atmospheric setting with candles, lotions, soap, and small home deco stuff. The shop is a less expensive alternative to Jo Malone.
www.eightsq.co.uk

Elemis
Luxurious skincare that combines the best of nature and science. Plus the spa treatments are heavenly.
www.elemis.com

Jo Malone
Mood setting done right: scented candles, bath oils, facials and home fragrance. All the inspiration a girl could ever want – at a price.
www.jomalone.co.uk

L'Occitane
Skincare, body and bath products, that come in delicious fruity and floral flavours. It has an old-fashioned French feel.
www.loccitane.co.uk

Laura Mercier
A range of natural, wearable make-up; the foundations and concealers are particularly well-loved for creating a 'flawless finish'.
www.lauramercier.com

MAC
A must for every make-up addict. Top quality products in every shade under the sun.
www.maccosmetics.co.uk

Molton Brown
Luxurious scented candles, bath and body products, and more.
www.moltonbrown.co.uk

PERFUMES

Nails Inc
A huge selection of on-trend nail colours.
www.nailsinc.com

The Organic Pharmacy
Using only 100% organic ingredients, these
products are free from harmful additives.
www.theorganicpharmacy.com

Origins
An excellent range of feel-good face and body
products.
www.origins.co.uk

Philosophy
Everything from serious skincare to luxurious
body products and fresh fragrances. Totally
irresistible!
www.philosphy.com

Space NK Apothecary
The mecca of beauty products, these stores sell
all the top quality make-up and skincare brands.
At the flagship London branch you can also
indulge in facials and massages.
www.spacenk.co.uk

Urban Decay
Cheap and cheerful make-up.
www.urbandecay.com

Yves Saint Laurent
Seriously chic make-up, and unbeatable palettes
each season.
www.ysl-parfums.com

Chanel
www.chanel.com

Commes Des Garçons
www.doverstreetmarket.com

Dior
www.dior.com

Jean Paul Gaultier
www.jeanpaul-gaultier.com

Lalique
www.cristallalique.fr
Available from Roja Dove Haute
Parfumerie at Harrods, London

Lanvin
www.lanvin.com

Marc Jacobs
www.marcjacobs.com

Perfumus Firenze
www.profumodifirenze.com
Available at Harrods, London

Stephen Burlingham
Available from Roja Dove Haute
Parfumerie at Harrods, London

Tom Ford
www.tomford.com

STOCKISTS

Bombshell

Susannah wears:
Pink gown – Coast
Long satin gloves – Angels & Berman's
www.fancydress.com
Fake fur wrap – Dior
Diamanté cuff – Mikey
Diamanté necklace – Mikey
Shoes – Silver Jimmy Choo.

On the mannequins L-R:
1: Striped shirt –Warehouse; Bra and skirt – both Marks & Spencer; Tights – Falke
2: Leopard dress – Diva; Cuff – vintage from Mensah
3: Red cardigan – oli.co.uk; Yellow floral blouse – from TK Maxx; Turned up jeans – Topshop
4: Check dress – Marc Jacobs; Belt – LK Bennett.

Charlotte wears:
Stripe top – Kaliko at John Lewis
Belt – Miss Selfridge
Pedal pushers – John Lewis
Gold shoes – New Look.
Black dress – Vintage from Beyond Retro
Black lace bra – Bravissimo
Black shoes – Monsoon.

Finishing touches:
White fake fur wrap – vintage from Mensah

www.mensah.co.uk
Earrings – Mikey
Shoes –Yves Saint Laurent
Bra – Wonderbra
Powder Puff – Benfit
Gold clutch bag – Anya Hindmarch
Red Lipstick – Chanel
Red Nail Varnish – Chanel
Diamanté cuff– vintage from Portobello Market
Hairspray – Elnett
Scent– Woman by Jean–Paul Gaultier.

Gamine

Trinny wears:
White dress – Prada
Yellow handbag – vintage from Portobello bag
Yellow shoes – Christian Louboutin
Sunglasses – Linda Farrow Vintage
www.lindafarrowvintage.com

On the mannequins L–R:
1: Purple dress – Fendi
2: Gold babydoll dress – Mayle
3: Yellow and white coat – vintage Courrèges from Mensah 020 8960 8520
4: Print skirt – Jaeger; yellow top with little beaded collar – River Island; Sequin hat – Marks & Spencer; belt – Jigsaw.

Pookie wears:
Black skirt – from TK Maxx;
Beige / white jumper and attached shirt – Monsoon
Shoes – French Sole
Belt – Marc Jacobs.
Burgundy lace dress – Lanvin
Tights – Falke at MyTights.com
Wedges – Marni
Earrings – vintage from Orsini.

Finishing touches:
Shoes – Miu Miu
Sunglasses – Linda Farrow Vintage
Head Band – Cherry Chau
Handbag – vintage from Portobello Bag
www.vickysleeper.com
Beret – River Island
Mascara –YSL False Lash Effect
Nail Varnish – nails inc
Body Lotion – Baby Grace by Philosophy
Bracelet – Trinny's own
Scent – Miss Dior Chérie by Dior.

Cutting Edge Cool

Susannah wears:
Cape – Vintage from Rellik
Leggings – American Apparel
Grey shirt – Cos
Grey suede stack shoes – Karen Millen

Belt – Jaeger

Earrings – Butler & Wilson.

Trinny wears:

Silver Dress – Vanessa Bruno

Pink Tights – Falke At
Mytights.Com

Purple Shoes – Marni

Platinum Wig – Juliet's 020
8838 4700.

On the mannequins L–R:

1: Yellow jacket and patterned
dress – both Jaeger

2: White chiffon blouse –
Chloé; Cropped jacket –
Topshop; Leggings –
American Apparel

3: Pink zip leggings – Topshop;
Gold beaded tunic – Prada;
Gold leather jacket – Karen
Millen

4: Orange t–shirt – Cos; Black
dress – Future Classics.

Natalie wears:

Camouflage silk jacket – All
Saints

Pink leggings – American
Apparel

Shoe boots – Topshop

Yellow bag – Marc Jacobs

Black wig – Juliet's 020 8838
4700.

Black embroidered dress –
Jaeger London

Turquoise belt – Fendi

Shoes – Moda in Pelle

Orange tights – Pretty Polly.

Finishing touches:

Tights – Pamela Mann at
mytights.com

Spider brooch – Butler &
Wilson

Leopard trilby – Prada

Earrings – Vintage

Nail Varnish – Nina Ultra Pro

Purple belt – vintage Paloma
Picasso

Sunglasses – AM Eyewear at
Browns Focus

Shoes – Aldo

Eye shadows – MAC

Scent – 'Truly' by Stephen
Burlingham, available from
Roja Dove Haute Parfumerie
at Harrods.

Androgyne

Susannah wears:

Skirt with braces – Alexander
McQueen

Shirt – D&G

Shoes – Pied a Terre.

Trinny wears:

White shirt – Balenciaga

Waistcoat – Marc Jacobs

Trousers – Balenciaga

Pendant on chain – Lanvin

On the mannequins L–R:

1: Long black and white bib

dress – Temperley

2: Blue grandad shirt dress –
Jigsaw; Black waistcoat –
Principles; Black skinny
jeans – Diesel

3: Long grey jacket –
Balenciaga; Trousers – by
Asuzana White shirt – Jil
Sander; Black tie – Topman

4: Black cigarette pants – Stella
McCartney for H&M; Black
tuxedo jacket – vintage Yves
Saint Laurent; Net
headpiece – Basia Zarzycka.

Rosamund wears:

White grandad shirt and beige
pinstripe suit – all Jaeger at
John Lewis

Black patent brogues – Bottega
Veneta

Trilby – Lola.

Black tuxedo coat – Trinny &
Susannah for Littlewoods
Direct

Black net skirt – vintage from
Portobello Road market

Ruffled white shirt – 1493

Tights, Pamela Mann

Shoes, Bottega Veneta.

Finishing touches:

Watch – Marks & Spencer

Cufflinks – Marks & Spencer

Hat – Jil Sander

Belt – Marks & Spencer

Socks – Falke at Mytights.com

Silk tie – Prada
Balm – Baume de Rose by Terry
Mineral powder – Laura
  Mercier
Eye & brow powder – Givenchy
Scent – 'Man 2' by Comme des
  Garçons.

Ice Queen

Susannah wears:
White & Gold Dress –
  Anglomania by Vivienne
  Westwood
Beige heels – Christian
  Louboutin.

Trinny wears:
Grey Jumper – Zara
Dress – Miu Miu
Shoes – Stella McCartney
Pearl Necklace – Butler &
  Wilson
Gloves – Vintage from The
  Shop, Cheshire St London
  E1.

On the mannequins L–R:
1: Grey flannel trousers – Miu
  Miu; Grey sweater –
  Inhabit; Grey fur shrug –
  Matthew Williamson; Pearls
  – Freedom at Topshop
2: Cream coat – Jesire
3: Lilac chiffon dress, Prada;
  Vintage hat – Beyond Retro
4: Silver cape – Allegra Hicks;
  Cream skirt – LK Bennett at

John Lewis; Belt – Marc
  Jacobs.
Charlotte wears:
Cream twin set and cream
  tweed skirt – both LK
  Bennett
Pearls – Butler & Wilson;
Shoes – Red Herring at
  Debenhams.
Silver linen mix dress and
  matching coat – Phase Eight
  at John Lewis
Shoes – Red Herring at
  Debenhams.

Finishing touches:
Bag – Anya Hindmarch
Shoes – LK Bennett
Gloves – Dents
Earrings – Bulter & Wilson
Watch – Marks & Spencer
Belt –Jigsaw
Pearls – Berganza
Lipstick, nail varnish, lip brush
  and eyebrow pencil – all by
  Dior
Scent – Chanel No 5.

Avant–Garde Eccentric

Susannah wears:
Black dress – Diva
Hat – Philip Treacy.

Trinny wears:
Velvet print dress – Vintage
  from Gray's Antique Market
Orange tights – Pamela Mann

at mytights.com
Feather cape – Butler & Wilson
Leopard print shoes – D&G
Orange beads – Dinosaur
  Designs
Turban – Prada
Big ring – Legge and Braine.

On the mannequins L–R:
1: Orange jersey top –
  Balenciaga; Patterned trousers
  – Missoni; Turban – Prada;
  Beads – Butler & Wilson
2: Yellow, white and black kaftan
  – Temperley. Necklace –
  Marni; Bangles – vintage
3: Brown dress with flowered
  hem – Pierre Cardin;
  Necklace – Marni; Hat –
  Topman; Tights – Jonathon
  Aston at www.mytights.com
4: Gold jumpsuit, emerald green
  blouse and necklace – all
  vintage from Rellik; Belt –
  Fendi; Marabou shrug –
  Tuleh, Sunglasses – Linda
  Farrow Vintage; Resin bangles
  – Dinosaur Designs
  www.dinosaurdesigns.com.au

Pookie wears:
Chinese jacket –
  lindawrigglesworth.com; Full
  skirt – Donna Karan; Tights –
  Emilio Cavallini; Belt –
  Fendi; Black shoes – Marni;
  Bangles – mixed vintage and

Angie Gooderham.
Tomato red chiffon dress,
vintage Ossie Clarke; Shoes –
Miu Miu; Ring – Legge and
Braine
www.leggeandbraine.com

Finishing touches:
Earrings – Collected by Trinny
in India
Breast plate – Frontiers 020
7727 6132
White Mosaic bag – Sam Ubhi
Rivera print bag – Prada
Vintage gold bag – Portobello
Bag
Vintage red bag – Portobello Bag
Gold quilted bag – Chanel
Shoes – Prada
Pink hat – Philip Treacy
Resin bangles – Dinosaur
Designs
www.dinosaurdesigns.com.au
Eye glitter – Urban decay
Lipsticks – MAC
Bindis – Ranjan Body Decor
from Southall Market
Scent – Arpège by Lanvin.

Diva
Susannah wears:
Long sequinned gown –
Temperley
Necklace – Butler & Wilson

Trinny wears:
Floral Dress – Prada

Shoes – Christian Louboutin
Grey fake fur shrug – Vintage
from Annie's Antiques 020
7359 0796
Cuff – Butler & Wilson
Silk rose – Johnny Loves Rosie

On the mannequins L–R:
1: Black pencil skirt – Diva;
Metallic shirt – Sara Berman
2: Leopard print coat – vintage
from One of a Kind; Black
dress – Diva; Brooch –
vintage from Butler & Wilson
3: Opera coat – Wallis – gloves
– vintage from Absolute
Vintage
4: Red and black beaded prom
dress – Trinny & Susannah
for Littlewoods Direct .

Natalie wears:
Yellow and black dress – Karen
Millen; Fishnets – Pretty
Polly; Shoes – Giuseppe
Zanotti
Turquoise strapless dress –
Monsoon; Feather shrug –
Christian Dior; Earrings –
collected by Trinny in India;
Silver shoes – Prada.

Finishing touches:
Black fur – Vintage from
Virginia
Marabou mules – Agent
Provocateur – Agent P

Cigarette holder – collected by
Trinny in Paris
Brooch – Butler & Wilson
Emerald and Diamond ring –
Berganza www.berganza.com
Shoes – Rochas
Earrings – Butler & Wilson
Gold clutch – Chanel
Black lace basque – La Senza
Fan – collected by Susannah in
Spain
Powder – Givenchy
Eye kohl and lipstick –
Guerlain
Rouge Noir nail varnish –
Chanel
Scent – 'Pearls de Lalique' by
Lalique Parfums, available
from Roja Dove Haute
Parfumerie at Harrods.

Sophisticate
Susannah wears:
Metallic shirt – Sara Berman
Trousers – Trinny and
Susannah for Littlewoods
Direct
Black belt – Jaeger
Necklace – Lanvin
Silver wig – Juliet's 020 8838
4700.

Trinny wears:
Grey wool dress –
Giambattista Vialli
White ruffled shirt – Diana
Von Furstenburg

Black jacket with sleeve puffs – Roksanda Ilincic
Black tights – Walford
Shoes – Stella McCartney
Black clutch bag – vintage from Portobello Bag
Black sunglasses – Chanel at David Clulow.

On the mannequins L–R:

1: Cream shirt – Monsoon Fusion; Black vintage skirt – The Shop, Cheshire St, E1
2: Pink satin coat – Gratzia Bagnaresi at A la Mode ; Pink floral shift dress – LK Bennett at John Lewis
3: Cream tweed skirt and jacket – Paul Costello collection at John Lewis; White blouse – Monsoon
4: Blue beaded satin dress – Prada.

Rosamund wears:

Black trousers – Trinny and Susannah for Littlewoods Direct; Belt – vintage from Annie's Antiques; Blouse – Diane Von Furstenberg; Shoes – Faith Solo by Gil Carvalho; Bag – Chanel
Black and white bib dress – Temperley; Shoes – Dune; Bakelite clutch bag – Mimco; Earrings and ring – both vintage from Butler & Wilson.

Finishing touches:

Silk Square – Louis Vuitton
Sunglasses – Prada at The Sunglasses Hut
Long metal and crystal chain – vintage Chanel from Grays Antique Market
Shoes – Christian Louboutin
Birkin – Hermes
Mimosa candle – Diptyque
Air brush foundation – SKII
'La Base' make–up primer by Lancôme
Scent – 'White Jasmine and Mint' by Jo Malone.

Rock Chick

Susannah wears:

Jeans – Superfine
Velvet Jacket – Zara
Black Top – Jaeger
Patent boots – Azzedine Alaia
Necklace – Lanvin.

Trinny wears:

Skull t–shirt – Alexander McQueen
Fake fur shrug – Fendi
Black jeans – Diesel
Shoes – Prada
Sequinned beret – Marks & Spencer.

On the mannequins L–R:

1: Striped jacket – Topshop; Striped cardigan – All Saints; Black mini skirt – Topshop; Big black bag – Topshop; White t–shirt – Cos; Sunglasses – RayBan; Neck scarf –
2: Leather jacket – Rick Owens; Lumberjack shirt – Topshop; Patterned t–shirt – All Saints; Jeans – Diesel
3: Cropped tuxedo jacket – Topshop; Dip–dyed t–shirt – All Saints; Belt, vintage from Betond Retro, Straw trilby – Topman ; Leggings – Trinny & Susannah Original Magic Knickers; Cross on chain – Butler & Wilson
4: Skirt – vintage from Absolute Vintage, Waistcoat – Warehouse; Leopard scarf – Louis Vuitton; Leather wristlets – Topman.

Charlotte wears:

Black tuxedo jacket – Stella McCartney for H&M; Leatherette jeans – Zara; Grey t–shirt (underneath) and dark grey pleated tunic – both All Saints; Biker boots – Frye; Scarf – Peekaboo at Topshop.
Black studded dress – Topshop; PVC leggings – American Apparel; Long necklace – Butler & Wilson; Short necklace – Topman; Bangle, Butler & Wilson; Bag –

vintage from Portobello Bag, Shoes Gil Carvelo Faith.

Finishing touches:
Studded shoes – Topshop
Black fingerless gloves – Dents
Scarf –Alexander McQeen
Boots –Yves Saint Laurent
Skull and crucifix necklace – Butler & Wilson
Leather tie – Topman
Sunglasses – Rayban Wayfarers
Rock Star belt – All Saints
Lipstick – Givenchy
Bad Gal kohl pencil – Benefit
Blue Satin nail varnish by Chanel
Hair powder – Bumble & bumble
Scent – 'Pure Poison' by Dior.

Minimalist
Susannah wears:
White shirt dress – Zara
Black pumps – French Sole
Red, white and blue bangles – Freedom at Topshop
Black wig – Juliet's 020 8838 4700.

Trinny wears:
Grey folded dress – Marni
Grey opaque tights – Falke at www.mytights.com
Purple wedge shoes – Marni
Resin bangle – Dinosaur Designs

Red wig – Juliet's 020 8838 4700.

On the mannequins L–R:
1: Black dress – Bottega Veneta
2: Nude top and electric blue skirt – both Marni; White bangle – Dinosaur Designs
3: Sculptural black jacket – Balenciaga; Black trousers – Chloé
4: Beige patent Mac and graphic print dress (underneath) – both Cos; Pink patent belt – Reiss.

Pookie wears:
White shirt with patent trim – 1493; Black cigarette pants – Stella McCartney for H&M; Blue mac – Prada; Cut–out wedge shoes – Nine West; Sunglasses – Linda Farrow vintage.
Blue silk top – Lanvin; Black puffball skirt – Alaia; Elastic shoes – Stella McCartney; Black tights – Jonathon Aston www.mytights.com

Finishing touches:
Silver shoes–Prada
Orange bone ring – collected in Brazil
Black necklace –Hoss Intropia
Small clutch – Jalda
Cleanser – Eve Lom

Eight hour cream – Elizabeth Arden
Foundation and concealer – Chantecaille
Red lipstick – NARS
Scent – 'Bois 1920 Vetiver Ambrato' by Perfumus Firenze.

High Maintenance
Susannah wears:
Orange satin dress – Karen Millen
Leopard print bag – Prada
Puprle and gold shoes – Christian Louboutin
Coloured crystal cuff – Butler & Wilson.

Trinny wears:
Cream dress – Prada
Gold Shoes – Prada
Crystal ring – Legge and Braine.

On the mannequins L–R:
1: White pencil skirt – Sticky Fingers at House of Fraser; Cream and white cardigan – Jesire at John Lewis; Birkin bag – Hermes; Sunglasses – Yves Saint Laurent at David Clulow; Necklace – Freedom at Topshop
2: Yellow dress – Collette Dinnigan; Bracelet – Butler & Wilson

3: Grey Mac – Karen Millen; White shirt – Nicole Farhi; Black trousers – Chloé; Trilby – vintage from Absolute Vintage; Belt – New Look

3: Long chiffon and crystal gown – Temperley.

Natalie wears:

White jacket – Jaeger London; Black shirt – Principles; Jeans – Karen Millen; Gold clutch bag – Chanel; Shoes – Christian Louboutin.

Grey dress – Diva; Yellow Mac – LK Bennett at John Lewis; Shoes – Dune; Tights – Falke; Sunglasses – Gucci at David Clulow; Birkin bag – Hermes.

Finishing touches:

Push up bra – BHS
Shoes – Christian Louboutin
Sunglasses – Versace from Sunglasses Hut
Tennis bracelet – EC One
Earrings – Lanvin
Watch – Rolex
Diamond ring – Boodles
Fake tan – St Tropez
Lip glosses – Dior
Bronzing powder – Lancome
Make–up jewel – Dior
Scent – 'Black Orchid' by Tom Ford.

Boho

Susannah wears:

Long print dress– Trinny and Susannah for Littlewoods Direct
Necklace – Chloé
Indian Bangles – Southall market.

Trinny wears:

Purple tiered dress – Balenciaga Silk
Pink silk top – Balenciaga
Necklace and bangles – collected in Brazil.

On the mannequins L–R:

1: Striped jacket – McQ by Alexander McQueen at TK Maxx; Scarf – Alexander McQueen; Jeans – Diesel; Top – Antik Batik; Hat – House of Fraser

2: Cream kaftan with beads, Rose Anne De Pampeloune; leggings, Zara; waistcoat, Marc Jacobs

3: Pink and blue silk strapless dress – Shanti; Necklace – Marni; Waistcoat – 12th Street by Cynthia Vincent; Sunglasses – Chanel

4: Black dress – See by Chloé at TK Maxx; Waistcoat – Kate Moss for Topshop; Necklace and bangles – treasurebox.co.uk

Rosamund wears:

Dark wide legged jeans – All Saints; Pirate shirt – Karen Millen; Suede waistcoat – Balenciaga; Necklace – Marni; Bangles – Dinosaur Designs and Treasurebox.co.uk; Shoes – Nicole Farhi.

Patterned beige and gold dress – Zac Posen; Gold crochet cardigan – Prada; Necklace – Marni; Opaque tights – Falke; Shoes – Nicole Farhi.

Finishing touches:

Sunglasses – Linda Farrow Vintage
Leather fringed bag – Antik Batik
Gladiator sandals – Kate Kuba
Indian bangles – Southall Market
Sequinned skull cap – Annie's Antiques
Lip gloss – Philosophy
Surf spray for hair – Bumble & bumble
Body Glow – NARS
Scent – 'Daisy' by Marc Jacobs.

PICTURE CREDITS

The publishers have made every effort
to contact and receive permission to use
all the images contained in this book
and shall, if notified, correct any errors,
oversights or omissions in subsequent
editions.

Bombshell (p. 18-9)

Michael Ochs Archives/Getty Images; Gail
Shumway/Getty Images; V&A Images
(wallpaper background).

Gamine (p. 38-9)

Michael Ochs Archives/Getty Images;
Potter/Getty Images; Time & Life
Pictures/Getty Images; Nic Taylor/Getty
Images; Niall Benvie/CORBIS; Jane
Miller/Getty Images; V&A Images (wallpaper
background).

Cutting Edge (p. 58-9)

Hans Gedda/Sygma/Corbis; Damian Hirst; Paul
Hawthorne/Rex Features; Simon
Matthews/FilmMagic/Getty Images; Kurt
Krieger/Corbis; Frans Lanting/Corbis; V&A
Images (wallpaper background).

Androgyne (p. 78-9)

Spike Powell/Elizabeth Whiting &
Associates/CORBIS; Arnaldo Magnani/Getty
Images; Brandtner & Staedeli/CORBIS;
Popperfoto/Getty Images; V&A Images
(wallpaper background).

Ice Queen (p. 98-9)

Time & Life Pictures/Getty Images; Kobal;
Rune Hellestad/CORBIS; Iconica/Getty
Images; The Bridgeman Art Library;
Photomorgana/CORBIS; Photodisc/Getty
Images; Tim Rooke/Rex Features; V&A Images
(wallpaper background).

Avant-Garde (p. 118-9)

Siede Preis/Getty Images; The Gallery
Collection/Corbis; Hulton Archive/Getty
Images; Sipa Press/Rex Features; Camera
Press/Debra Hurford Brown; Getty Images;
Georgios Kefalas/epa/Corbis; V&A Images
(wallpaper background).

Diva (p. 138-9)

Sharok Hatami/Rex Features; Hulton
Archive/Getty Images; John Kobal
Foundation/Getty Images; Condé Nast
Archive/CORBIS; ????; Arno
Burgi/epa/CORBIS; The Bridgeman Art
Library; WireImage/Getty Images; V&A Images
(wallpaper background).

Sophisticate (p. 158-9)

Time & Life Pictures/Getty Images; Roger
Viollet/Getty Images; Kevin Muggleton/
CORBIS; Geoffrey Clements/CORBIS; Hulton
Archive/Getty Images; Bettmann/CORBIS;
Sipa Press/Rex Features; Getty Images;
Bettmann/CORBIS; V&A Images (wallpaper
background).

Rock Chick (p. 178-9)

Sheila Rock/Rex Features; Stockbyte/Getty Images; Getty Images; Terry O'Neill/Getty Images; Martin Harvey/Getty Images; Jefferson Hayman/CORBIS; Bettmann/CORBIS; Joel Brodsky/CORBIS; Brian Rasic/Rex Features; V&A Images (wallpaper background).

Minimalist (p. 198-9)

Time & Life Pictures/Getty Images; The Bridgeman Art Library; Marcel Hartmann/Sygma/CORBIS; AFP/Getty Images; Nils Jorgensen/Rex Features; WireImage/Getty Images; V&A (wallpaper background).

High Maintenance (p. 218-9)

Most Wanted/Rex Features; Alex Segre/Alamy; Niall Benvie/CORBIS; Marion Curtis/Rex Features; FilmMagic/Getty Images; Steve Sands/New York Newswire/CORBIS; Paul Hurd/Getty Images; John Gress/Reuters/CORBIS; V&A Images (wallpaper background).

Boho (p. 238-9)

Hulton Archive/Getty Images; DMA/Alamy; Richard Young/Rex Features; WireImage/Getty Images; Douglas Menuez/Getty Images; akg-images/Archives CDA/Guillo; V&A Images (wallpaper background).

Jacket and cover images

Photographs of Trinny & Susannah by Robin Matthews. Grace Kelly (Time & Life Pictures/Getty Images), Gwen Stefani (Kurt Krieger/Corbis) and Marlene Dietrich (Popperfoto/Getty Images). V&A (wallpaper background). Seven-spotted ladybird Niall Benvie/Corbis.

ACKNOWLEDGEMENTS

And loving thanks to Sten and Jonny, forever in our lives.

Photography by Robin Matthews, using a throw-away camera.
Assisted by Gemma Spears.

Make-up by Charlotte Ribeyro, using Dulux.
Additional make-up by Vale.

Hair
Jennie Roberts, using a dog comb.
Additional hair Liz Taw and Devon Whyte.
Assisted by Saynab Awelah and Vernon Francois @ nakedartists.com

Wardrobe supervision
Annie Swain, using Cellotape and safety pins.
Erica Davies, using magic.
Assisted by Sophie Kirkwood and Lois Strouthos.

Directory research
Victoria Shaddick.
Additional research by Ella Porter.

Illustrations by Emil Dacanay and Sian Rance at D.R. ink.
Hair and make-up illustrations by Jessie Ford.

Writing coordination and research
Jessica Jones

Models
Natalie MacKenzie
Pookie Shaddick
Charlotte Paterson
Rosamund Payne

Special thanks to
Michael Foster for his enduring short temper.
Cheryl Konteh for being there always.
Susan Haynes for being gently persuasive.
David Rowley for his creativity and stubbornness.
Jenny and Gemma, for keeping our kids safe and happy.